ISEE UPPER LEVEL MATH FOR BEGINNERS

The Ultimate Step by Step Guide to Preparing for the ISEE Upper Level Math Test

By

Reza Nazari

About Effortless Math Education

Effortless Math Education operates the www.effortlessmath.com website, which prepares and publishes Test prep and Mathematics learning resources. Effortless Math authors' team strives to prepare and publish the best quality Mathematics learning resources to make learning Math easier for all. We Help Students Learn to Love Mathematics.

All inquiries should be addressed to:
info@effortlessMath.com
www.EffortlessMath.com

ISBN: 978-1-64612-947-8

Published by: **Effortless Math Education Inc**

for Online Math Practice Visit www.EffortlessMath.com

Welcome to
ISEE Upper Level Math Prep
2023

Thank you for choosing Effortless Math for your ISEE Upper Level Math test preparation and congratulations on making the decision to take the ISEE Upper Level test! It's a remarkable move you are taking, one that shouldn't be diminished in any capacity. That's why you need to use every tool possible to ensure you succeed on the test with the highest possible score, and this extensive study guide is one such tool.

This book will help you prepare for (and even ACE) the ISEE Upper Level test's math section. As test day draws nearer, effective preparation becomes increasingly more important. Thankfully, you have this comprehensive study guide to help you get ready for the test. With this guide, you can feel confident that you will be more than ready for the ISEE Upper Level Math test when the time comes.

First and foremost, it is important to note that this book is a study guide and not a textbook. It is best read from cover to cover. Every lesson of this "self-guided math book" was carefully developed to ensure that you are making the most effective use of your time while preparing for the test. This up-to-date guide reflects the 2023 test guidelines and will put you on the right track to hone your math skills, overcome exam anxiety, and boost your confidence, so that you can have your best to succeed on the ISEE Upper Level Math test.

This study guide will:

☑ Explain the format of the ISEE Upper Level Math test.

☑ Describe specific test-taking strategies that you can use on the test.

☑ Provide ISEE Upper Level Math test-taking tips.

☑ Review all ISEE Upper Level Math concepts and topics you will be tested on.

☑ Help you identify the areas in which you need to concentrate your study time.

☑ Offer exercises that help you develop the basic math skills you will learn in each section.

☑ Give **2 realistic and full-length practice tests** (featuring new question types) with detailed answers to help you measure your exam readiness and build confidence.

This resource contains everything you will ever need to succeed on the ISEE Upper Level Math test. You'll get in-depth instructions on every math topic as well as tips and techniques on how to answer each question type. You'll also get plenty of practice questions to boost your test-taking confidence.

In addition, in the following pages you'll find:

➢ **How to Use This Book Effectively** – This section provides you with step-by-step instructions on how to get the most out of this comprehensive study guide.

➢ **How to study for the ISEE Upper Level Math Test** – A six-step study program has been developed to help you make the best use of this book and prepare for your ISEE

Upper Level Math test. Here you'll find tips and strategies to guide your study program and help you understand ISEE Upper Level Math and how to ace the test.

➤ **ISEE Upper Level Math Review** – Learn everything you need to know about the ISEE Upper Level Math test.

➤ **ISEE Upper Level Math Test-Taking Strategies** – Learn how to effectively put these recommended test-taking techniques into use for improving your ISEE Upper Level Math score.

➤ **Test Day Tips** – Review these tips to make sure you will do your best when the big day comes.

Effortless Math's ISEE Upper Level Online Center

Effortless Math Online ISEE Upper Level Center offers a complete study program, including the following:

✓ Step-by-step instructions on how to prepare for the ISEE Upper Level Math test

✓ Numerous ISEE Math worksheets to help you measure your math skills

✓ Complete list of ISEE Math formulas

✓ Video lessons for all ISEE Math topics

✓ Full-length ISEE Upper Level Math practice tests

✓ And much more…

No Registration Required.

Visit effortlessmath.com/ISEE to find your online ISEE Upper Level Math resources.

How to Use This Book Effectively

Look no further when you need a study guide to improve your math skills to succeed on the math portion of the ISEE Upper Level test. Each chapter of this comprehensive guide to the ISEE Upper Level Math will provide you with the knowledge, tools, and understanding needed for every topic covered on the test.

It's imperative that you understand each topic before moving onto another one, as that's the way to guarantee your success. Each topic provides you with examples and a step-by-step guide of every concept to better understand the content that will be on the test. To get the best possible results from this book:

➢ **Begin studying long before your test date**. This provides you ample time to learn the different math concepts. The earlier you begin studying for the test, the sharper your skills will be. Do not procrastinate! Provide yourself with plenty of time to learn the concepts and feel comfortable that you understand them when your test date arrives.

➢ **Practice consistently**. Study ISEE Upper Level Math concepts at least 20 to 30 minutes a day. Remember, slow and steady wins the race, which can be applied to preparing for the ISEE Upper Level Math test. Instead of cramming to tackle everything at once, be patient and learn the math topics in short bursts.

➢ Whenever you get a math problem wrong, **mark it off, and review it later** to make sure you understand the concept.

➢ Start each session by **looking over the previous material.**

➢ Once you've reviewed the book's lessons, **take the practice test at the back of the book** to gauge your level of readiness. Then, review your results. Read detailed answers and solutions for each question you missed.

➢ **Take another practice test** to get an idea of how ready you are to take the actual exam. Taking the practice tests will give you the confidence you need on test day. Simulate the ISEE Upper Level testing environment by sitting in a quiet room free from distraction. Make sure to clock yourself with a timer.

How to Study for the ISEE Upper Level Math Test

Studying for the ISEE Upper Level Math test can be a really daunting and boring task. What's the best way to go about it? Is there a certain study method that works better than others? Well, studying for the ISEE Upper Level Math can be done effectively. The following six-step program has been designed to make preparing for the ISEE Upper Level Math test more efficient and less overwhelming.

Step **1** - Create a study plan
Step **2** - Choose your study resources
Step **3** - Review, Learn, Practice
Step **4** - Learn and practice test-taking strategies
Step **5** - Learn the ISEE Upper Level Test format and take practice tests
Step **6** - Analyze your performance

STEP 1: Create a Study Plan

It's always easier to get things done when you have a plan. Creating a study plan for the ISEE Upper Level Math test can help you to stay on track with your studies. It's important to sit down and prepare a study plan with what works with your life, work, and any other obligations you may have. Devote enough time each day to studying.

It's also a great idea to break down each section of the exam into blocks and study one concept at a time.

It's important to understand that there is no "right" way to create a study plan. Your study plan will be personalized based on your specific needs and learning style.

Follow these guidelines to create an effective study plan for your ISEE Upper Level Math test:

★ **Analyze your learning style and study habits** – Everyone has a different learning style. It is essential to embrace your individuality and the unique way you learn. Think about what works and what doesn't work for you. Do you prefer ISEE Upper Level Math prep books or a combination of textbooks and video lessons? Does it work better for you if you study every night for thirty minutes or is it more effective to study in the morning before going to school?

★ **Evaluate your schedule** – Review your current schedule and find out how much time you can consistently devote to ISEE Upper Level Math study.

★ **Develop a schedule** – Now it's time to add your study schedule to your calendar like any other obligation. Schedule time for study, practice, and review. Plan out which topic you will study on which day to ensure that you're devoting enough time to each concept. Develop a study plan that is mindful, realistic, and flexible.

★ **Stick to your schedule** – A study plan is only effective when it is followed consistently. You should try to develop a study plan that you can follow for the length of your study program.

★ **Evaluate your study plan and adjust as needed** – Sometimes you need to adjust your plan when you have new commitments. Check in with yourself regularly to make sure that you're not falling behind in your study plan. Remember, the most important thing is sticking to your plan. Your study plan is all about helping you be more productive. If you find that your study plan is not as effective as you want, don't get discouraged. It's okay to make changes as you figure out what works best for you.

STEP 2: Choose Your Study Resources

There are numerous textbooks and online resources available for the ISEE Upper Level Math test, and it may not be clear where to begin. Don't worry! This study guide provides everything you need to fully prepare for your ISEE Upper Level Math test. In addition to the book content, you can also use Effortless Math's online resources. (video lessons, worksheets, formulas, etc.) On each page, there is a

link (and a QR code) to an online webpage which provides a comprehensive review of the topic, step-by-step instruction, video tutorial, and numerous examples and exercises to help you fully understand the concept.

You can also visit EffortlessMath.com/ISEE to find your online ISEE Upper Level Math resources.

STEP 3: Review, Learn, Practice

This ISEE Upper Level Math study guide breaks down each subject into specific skills or content areas. For instance, the percent concept is separated into different topics–percent calculation, percent increase and decrease, percent problems, etc. Use this study guide and Effortless Math online ISEE Upper Level center to help you go over all key math concepts and topics on the ISEE Upper Level Math test.

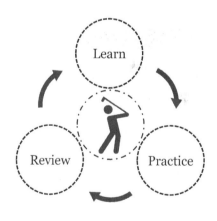

As you read each topic, take notes or highlight the concepts you would like to go over again in the future. If you're unfamiliar with a topic or something is difficult for you, use the link (or the QR code) at the bottom of the page to find the webpage that provides more instruction about that topic. For each math topic, plenty of instructions, step-by-step guides, and examples are provided to ensure you get a good grasp of the material.

Quickly review the topics you do understand to get a brush-up of the material. Be sure to do the practice questions provided at the end of every chapter to measure your understanding of the concepts.

STEP 4: Learn and Practice Test-taking Strategies

In the following sections, you will find important test-taking strategies and tips that can help you earn extra points. You'll learn how to think strategically and when to guess if you don't know the answer to a question. Using ISEE Upper Level Math test-taking strategies and tips can help you raise your score and do well on the test. Apply test taking strategies on the practice tests to help you boost your confidence.

STEP 5: Learn the ISEE Upper Level Test Format and Take Practice Tests

The ISEE Upper Level *Test Review* section provides information about the structure of the ISEE Upper Level test. Read this section to learn more about the ISEE Upper Level test structure, different test sections, the number of questions in each section, and the section time limits. When you have a prior understanding of the test format and different types of ISEE Upper Level Math questions, you'll feel more confident when you take the actual exam.

Once you have read through the instructions and lessons and feel like you are ready to go – take advantage of both of the full-length ISEE Upper Level Math practice tests available in this study guide. Use the practice tests to sharpen your skills and build confidence.

The ISEE Upper Level Math practice tests offered at the end of the book are formatted similarly to the actual ISEE Upper Level Math test. When you take each practice test, try to simulate actual testing conditions. To take the practice tests, sit in a quiet space, time yourself, and work through as many of the questions as time allows. The practice tests are followed by detailed answer explanations to help you find your weak areas, learn from your mistakes, and raise your ISEE Upper Level Math score.

Step 6: Analyze Your Performance

After taking the practice tests, look over the answer keys and explanations to learn which questions you answered correctly and which you did not. Never be discouraged if you make a few mistakes. See them as a learning opportunity. This will highlight your strengths and weaknesses.

You can use the results to determine if you need additional practice or if you are ready to take the actual ISEE Upper Level Math test.

Looking for more?

Visit effortlessmath.com/ISEE to find hundreds of ISEE Upper Level Math worksheets, video tutorials, practice tests, ISEE Upper Level Math formulas, and much more.

Or scan this QR code.

No Registration Required.

ISEE Upper Level Test Review

The Independent School Entrance Exam (ISEE) is a standardized test developed by the Educational Records Bureau for its member schools as part of their admission process.

- There are currently four Levels of the ISEE:
- Primary Level (entering Grades 2 - 4)
- Lower Level (entering Grades 5 and 6)
- Middle Level (entering Grades 7 and 8)
- Upper Level (entering Grades 9 - 12)

There are five sections on the ISEE Upper Level Test:

- Verbal Reasoning
- Quantitative Reasoning
- Reading Comprehension
- Mathematics Achievement
- and a 30-minute essay

ISEE Upper Level tests use a multiple-choice format and contain two Mathematics sections:

Quantitative Reasoning

There are 37 questions in the Quantitative Reasoning section and students have 35 minutes to answer the questions. This section contains word problems and quantitative comparisons. The word problems require either no calculation or simple calculation. The quantitative comparison items present two quantities, (A) and (B), and the student needs to select one of the following four answer choices:

(A) The quantity in Column A is greater.

(B) The quantity in Column B is greater.

(C) The two quantities are equal.

(D) The relationship cannot be determined from the information given.

Mathematics Achievement

There are 47 questions in the Mathematics Achievement section and students have 40 minutes to answer the questions. Mathematics Achievement measures students' knowledge of Mathematics requiring one or more steps in calculating the answer.

In this book, there are two complete ISEE Upper Level Quantitative Reasoning and Mathematics Achievement Tests. Let your student take these tests to see what score they will be able to receive on a real ISEE Upper Level test.

ISEE Upper Level Math Test-Taking Strategies

Here are some test-taking strategies that you can use to maximize your performance and results on the ISEE Upper Level Math test.

#1 : USE THIS APPROACH TO ANSWER EVERY ISEE UPPER LEVEL MATH QUESTION

- Review the question to identify keywords and important information.

- Translate the keywords into math operations so you can solve the problem.

- Review the answer choices. What are the differences between answer choices?

- Draw or label a diagram if needed.

- Try to find patterns.

- Find the right method to answer the question. Use straightforward math, plug in numbers, or test the answer choices (backsolving).

- Double-check your work.

#2 : USE EDUCATED GUESSING

This approach is applicable to the problems you understand to some degree but cannot solve using straightforward math. In such cases, try to filter out as many answer choices as possible before picking an answer. In cases where you don't have a clue about what a certain problem entails, don't waste any time trying to eliminate answer choices. Just choose one randomly before moving onto the next question.

As you can ascertain, direct solutions are the most optimal approach. Carefully read through the question, determine what the solution is using the math you have learned before, then coordinate the answer with one of the choices available to you. Are you stumped? Make your best guess, then move on.

Don't leave any fields empty! Even if you're unable to work out a problem, strive to answer it. Take a guess if you have to. You will not lose points by getting an answer wrong, though you may gain a point by getting it correct!

#3: BALLPARK

A ballpark answer is a rough approximation. When we become overwhelmed by calculations and figures, we end up making silly mistakes. A decimal that is moved by one unit can change an answer from right to wrong, regardless of the number of steps that you went through to get it. That's where ballparking can play a big part.

If you think you know what the correct answer may be (even if it's just a ballpark answer), you'll usually have the ability to eliminate a couple of choices. While answer choices are usually based on the average student error and/or values that are closely tied, you will still be able to weed out choices that are way far afield. Try to find answers that aren't in the proverbial ballpark when you're looking for a wrong answer on a multiple-choice question. This is an optimal approach to eliminating answers to a problem.

#4: BACKSOLVING

A majority of questions on the ISEE Upper Level Math test will be in multiple-choice format. Many test-takers prefer multiple-choice questions, as at least the answer is right there. You'll typically have four answers to pick from. You simply need to figure out which one is correct. Usually, the best way to go about doing so is "backsolving."

As mentioned earlier, direct solutions are the most optimal approach to answering a question. Carefully read through a problem, calculate a solution, then correspond the answer with one of the choices displayed in front of you. If you can't calculate a solution, your next best approach involves "backsolving."

When backsolving a problem, contrast one of your answer options against the problem you are asked, then see which of them is most relevant. More often than not, answer choices are listed in ascending or descending order. In such cases, try out the choices B or C. If it's not correct, you can go either down or up from there.

#5 : Plugging In Numbers

"Plugging in numbers" is a strategy that can be applied to a wide range of different math problems on the ISEE Upper Level Math test. This approach is typically used to simplify a challenging question so that it is more understandable. By using the strategy carefully, you can find the answer without too much trouble.

The concept is fairly straightforward–replace unknown variables in a problem with certain values. When selecting a number, consider the following:

- Choose a number that's basic (just not too basic). Generally, you should avoid choosing 1 (or even 0). A decent choice is 2.

- Try not to choose a number that is displayed in the problem.

- Make sure you keep your numbers different if you need to choose at least two of them.

- More often than not, choosing numbers merely lets you filter out some of your answer choices. As such, don't just go with the first choice that gives you the right answer.

- If several answers seem correct, then you'll need to choose another value and try again. This time, though, you'll just need to check choices that haven't been eliminated yet.

- If your question contains fractions, then a potential right answer may involve either an LCD (least common denominator) or an LCD multiple.

- 100 is the number you should choose when you are dealing with problems involving percentages.

ISEE Upper Level Math – Test Day Tips

After practicing and reviewing all the math concepts you've been taught, and taking some ISEE Upper Level mathematics practice tests, you'll be prepared for test day. Consider the following tips to be extra-ready come test time.

Before Your Test...

What to do the night before:

- **Relax!** One day before your test, study lightly or skip studying altogether. You shouldn't attempt to learn something new, either. There are plenty of reasons why studying the evening before a big test can work against you. Put it this way–a marathoner wouldn't go out for a sprint before the day of a big race. Mental marathoners–such as yourself–should not study for any more than one hour 24 hours before a ISEE Upper Level test. That's because your brain requires some rest to be at its best. The night before your exam, spend some time with family or friends, or read a book.

- **Avoid bright screens** - You'll have to get some good shuteye the night before your test. Bright screens (such as the ones coming from your laptop, TV, or mobile device) should be avoided altogether. Staring at such a screen will keep your brain up, making it hard to drift asleep at a reasonable hour.

- **Make sure your dinner is healthy** - The meal that you have for dinner should be nutritious. Be sure to drink plenty of water as well. Load up on your complex carbohydrates, much like a marathon runner would do. Pasta, rice, and potatoes are ideal options here, as are vegetables and protein sources.

- **Get your bag ready for test day** - The night prior to your test, pack your bag with your stationery, admissions pass, ID, and any other gear that you need. Keep the bag right by your front door.

- **Make plans to reach the testing site** - Before going to sleep, ensure that you understand precisely how you will arrive at the site of the test. If parking is something you'll have to find first, plan for it. If you're dependent on public transit, then review the schedule. You should also make sure that the train/bus/subway/streetcar you use will be running. Find out about road closures as well. If a parent or friend is accompanying you, ensure that they understand what steps they have to take as well.

The Day of the Test

- **Get up reasonably early, but not too early.**

- **Have breakfast** - Breakfast improves your concentration, memory, and mood. As such, make sure the breakfast that you eat in the morning is healthy. The last thing you want to be is distracted by a grumbling tummy. If it's not your own stomach making those noises, another test taker close to you might be instead. Prevent discomfort or embarrassment by consuming a healthy breakfast. Bring a snack with you if you think you'll need it.

- **Follow your daily routine** - Do you watch TV each morning while getting ready for the day? Don't break your usual habits on the day of the test. Likewise, if coffee isn't something you drink in the morning, then don't take up the habit hours before your test. Routine consistency lets you concentrate on the main objective–doing the best you can on your test.

- **Wear layers** - Dress yourself up in comfortable layers. You should be ready for any kind of internal temperature. If it gets too warm during the test, take a layer off.

- **Get there on time** - The last thing you want to do is get to the test site late. Rather, you should be there 45 minutes prior to the start of the test. Upon your arrival, try not to hang out with anybody who is nervous. Any anxious energy they exhibit shouldn't influence you.

- **Leave the books at home** - No books should be brought to the test site. If you start developing anxiety before the test, books could encourage you to do some last-minute studying, which will only hinder you. Keep the books far away–better yet, leave them at home.

- **Make your voice heard** - If something is off, speak to a proctor. If medical attention is needed or if you'll require anything, consult the proctor prior to the start of the test. Any doubts you have should be clarified. You should be entering the test site with a state of mind that is completely clear.

- **Have faith in yourself** - When you feel confident, you will be able to perform at your best. When you are waiting for the test to begin, envision yourself receiving an outstanding result. Try to see yourself as someone who knows all the answers, no matter what the questions are. A lot of athletes tend to use this technique–particularly before a big competition. Your expectations will be reflected by your performance.

During your test

- **Be calm and breathe deeply** - You need to relax before the test, and some deep breathing will go a long way to help you do that. Be confident and calm. You got this. Everybody feels a little stressed out just before an evaluation of any kind is set to begin. Learn some effective breathing exercises. Spend a minute meditating before the test starts. Filter out any negative thoughts you have. Exhibit confidence when having such thoughts.

- **Concentrate on the test** - Refrain from comparing yourself to anyone else. You shouldn't be distracted by the people near you or random noise. Concentrate exclusively on the test. If you find yourself irritated by surrounding noises, earplugs can be used to block sounds off close to you. Don't forget–the test is going to last several hours if you're taking more than one subject of the test. Some of that time will be dedicated to brief sections. Concentrate on the specific section you are working on during a particular moment. Do not let your mind wander off to upcoming or previous sections.

- **Skip challenging questions** - Optimize your time when taking the test. Lingering on a single question for too long will work against you. If you don't know what the answer is to a certain question, use your best guess, and mark the question so you can review it later on. There is no need to spend time attempting to solve something you aren't sure about. That time would be better served handling the questions you can actually answer well. You will not be penalized for getting the wrong answer on a test like this.

- **Try to answer each question individually** - Focus only on the question you are working on. Use one of the test-taking strategies to solve the problem. If you aren't able to come up with an answer, don't get frustrated. Simply skip that question, then move onto the next one.

- **Don't forget to breathe!** Whenever you notice your mind wandering, your stress levels boosting, or frustration brewing, take a thirty-second break. Shut your eyes, drop your pencil, breathe deeply, and let your shoulders relax. You will end up being more productive when you allow yourself to relax for a moment.

- **Review your answer**. If you still have time at the end of the test, don't waste it. Go back and check over your answers. It is worth going through the test from start to finish to ensure that you didn't make a sloppy mistake somewhere.

- **Optimize your breaks** - When break time comes, use the restroom, have a snack, and reactivate your energy for the subsequent section. Doing some stretches can help stimulate your blood flow.

After your test

- **Take it easy** - You will need to set some time aside to relax and decompress once the test has concluded. There is no need to stress yourself out about what you could've said, or what you may have done wrong. At this point, there's nothing you can do about it. Your energy and time would be better spent on something that will bring you happiness for the remainder of your day.

■ **Redoing the test** - Did you pass the test? Congratulations! Your hard work paid off! Passing this test means that you are now as knowledgeable as somebody who has graduated high school.

If you have failed your test, though, don't worry! The test can be retaken. In such cases, you will need to follow the retake policy established by your state. You also need to re-register to take the exam again.

Contents

CHAPTER

1 Fractions and Mixed Numbers

Math topics that you'll learn in this chapter:

- ☑ Simplifying Fractions
- ☑ Adding and Subtracting Fractions
- ☑ Multiplying and Dividing Fractions
- ☑ Adding Mixed Numbers
- ☑ Subtracting Mixed Numbers
- ☑ Multiplying Mixed Numbers
- ☑ Dividing Mixed Numbers

1

Simplifying Fractions

- A fraction contains two numbers separated by a bar between them. The bottom number, called the denominator, is the total number of equally divided portions in one whole. The top number, called the numerator, is how many portions you have. And the bar represents the operation of division.

- Simplifying a fraction means reducing it to the lowest terms. To simplify a fraction, evenly divide both the top and bottom of the fraction by $2, 3, 5, 7$, etc.

- Continue until you can't go any further.

Examples:

Example 1. Simplify $\frac{18}{30}$

Solution: To simplify $\frac{18}{30}$, find a number that both 18 and 30 are divisible by. Both are divisible by 6. Then: $\frac{18}{30} = \frac{18 \div 6}{30 \div 6} = \frac{3}{5}$

Example 2. Simplify $\frac{40}{80}$

Solution: To simplify $\frac{48}{80}$, find a number that both 48 and 80 are divisible by. Both are divisible by 8 and 16. Then: $\frac{48}{80} = \frac{48 \div 8}{80 \div 8} = \frac{6}{10}$, 6 and 10 are divisible by 2, then: $\frac{6}{10} = \frac{3}{5}$ or $\frac{48}{80} = \frac{48 \div 16}{80 \div 16} = \frac{3}{5}$

Example 3. Simplify $\frac{40}{120}$

Solution: To simplify $\frac{40}{120}$, find a number that both 40 and 120 are divisible by. Both are divisible by 40, then: $\frac{40}{120} = \frac{40 \div 40}{120 \div 40} = \frac{1}{3}$

Adding and Subtracting Fractions

- For "like" fractions (fractions with the same denominator), add or subtract the numerators (top numbers) and write the answer over the common denominator (bottom numbers).

- Adding and Subtracting fractions with the same denominator:

- $$\frac{a}{b} + \frac{c}{b} = \frac{a+c}{b} \qquad \frac{a}{b} - \frac{c}{b} = \frac{a-c}{b}$$

- Find equivalent fractions with the same denominator before you can add or subtract fractions with different denominators.

- Adding and Subtracting fractions with different denominators:

$$\frac{a}{b} + \frac{c}{d} = \frac{ad+bc}{bd} \qquad \frac{a}{b} - \frac{c}{d} = \frac{ad-bc}{bd}$$

Examples:

Example 4. Find the sum. $\frac{2}{3} + \frac{1}{2} =$

Solution: These two fractions are "unlike" fractions. (they have different denominators). Use this formula: $\frac{a}{b} + \frac{c}{d} = \frac{ad+cb}{bd}$

Then: $\frac{2}{3} + \frac{1}{2} = \frac{(2)(2)+(3)(1)}{3 \times 2} = \frac{4+3}{6} = \frac{7}{6}$

Example 5. Find the difference. $\frac{3}{5} - \frac{2}{7} =$

Solution: For "unlike" fractions, find equivalent fractions with the same denominator before you can add or subtract fractions with different denominators. Use this formula:

$\frac{a}{b} - \frac{c}{d} = \frac{ad-bc}{bd}$

$\frac{3}{5} - \frac{2}{7} = \frac{(3)(7)-(2)(5)}{5 \times 7} = \frac{21-10}{35} = \frac{11}{35}$

Multiplying and Dividing Fractions

- Multiplying fractions: multiply the top numbers and multiply the bottom numbers. Simplify if necessary. $\frac{a}{b} \times \frac{c}{d} = \frac{a \times c}{b \times d}$

- Dividing fractions: Keep, Change, Flip

- Keep the first fraction, change the division sign to multiplication, and flip the numerator and denominator of the second fraction. Then, solve!

$$\frac{a}{b} \div \frac{c}{d} = \frac{a}{b} \times \frac{d}{c} = \frac{a \times d}{b \times c}$$

Examples:

Example 1. Multiply. $\frac{2}{3} \times \frac{3}{5} =$

Solution: Multiply the top numbers and multiply the bottom numbers.
$\frac{2}{3} \times \frac{3}{5} = \frac{2 \times 3}{3 \times 5} = \frac{6}{15}$

Example 2. Solve. $\frac{3}{4} \div \frac{2}{5} =$

Solution: Keep the first fraction, change the division sign to multiplication, and flip the numerator and denominator of the second fraction.
Then: $\frac{3}{4} \div \frac{2}{5} = \frac{3}{4} \times \frac{5}{2} = \frac{3 \times 5}{4 \times 2} = \frac{15}{8}$

Example 3. Calculate. $\frac{4}{5} \times \frac{3}{4} =$

Solution: Multiply the top numbers and multiply the bottom numbers.
$\frac{4}{5} \times \frac{3}{4} = \frac{4 \times 3}{5 \times 4} = \frac{12}{20}$, simplify: $\frac{12}{20} = \frac{12 \div 4}{20 \div 4} = \frac{3}{5}$

Example 4. Solve. $\frac{5}{6} \div \frac{3}{7} =$

Solution: Keep the first fraction, change the division sign to multiplication, and flip the numerator and denominator of the second fraction.
Then: $\frac{5}{6} \div \frac{3}{7} = \frac{5}{6} \times \frac{7}{3} = \frac{5 \times 7}{6 \times 3} = \frac{35}{18}$

Adding Mixed Numbers

Use the following steps for adding mixed numbers:

- Add whole numbers of the mixed numbers.

- Add the fractions of the mixed numbers.

- Find the Least Common Denominator (LCD) if necessary.

- Add whole numbers and fractions.

- Write your answer in lowest terms.

Examples:

Example 1. Add mixed numbers. $2\frac{1}{2} + 1\frac{2}{3} =$

Solution: Let's rewriting our equation with parts separated, $2\frac{1}{2} + 1\frac{2}{3} = 2 + \frac{1}{2} + 1 + \frac{2}{3}$. Now, add whole number parts: $2 + 1 = 3$

Add the fraction parts $\frac{1}{2} + \frac{2}{3}$. Rewrite to solve with the equivalent fractions. $\frac{1}{2} + \frac{2}{3} = \frac{3}{6} + \frac{4}{6} = \frac{7}{6}$. The answer is an improper fraction (numerator is bigger than denominator). Convert the improper fraction into a mixed number: $\frac{7}{6} = 1\frac{1}{6}$. Now, combine the whole and fraction parts: $3 + 1\frac{1}{6} = 4\frac{1}{6}$

Example 2. Find the sum. $1\frac{3}{4} + 2\frac{1}{2} =$

Solution: Rewriting our equation with parts separated, $1 + \frac{3}{4} + 2 + \frac{1}{2}$. Add the whole number parts:

$1 + 2 = 3$. Add the fraction parts: $\frac{3}{4} + \frac{1}{2} = \frac{3}{4} + \frac{2}{4} = \frac{5}{4}$

Convert the improper fraction into a mixed number: $\frac{5}{4} = 1\frac{1}{4}$.

Now, combine the whole and fraction parts: $3 + 1\frac{1}{4} = 4\frac{1}{4}$

bit.ly/2M4oABB
Find more at

Subtract Mixed Numbers

Use these steps for subtracting mixed numbers.

- Convert mixed numbers into improper fractions. $a\frac{c}{b} = \frac{ab+c}{b}$

- Find equivalent fractions with the same denominator for unlike fractions. (fractions with different denominators)

- Subtract the second fraction from the first one. $\frac{a}{b} - \frac{c}{d} = \frac{ad-bc}{bd}$

- Write your answer in lowest terms.

- If the answer is an improper fraction, convert it into a mixed number.

Examples:

Example 1. Subtract. $2\frac{1}{3} - 1\frac{1}{2} =$

Solution: Convert mixed numbers into fractions: $2\frac{1}{3} = \frac{2\times3+1}{3} = \frac{7}{3}$ and $1\frac{1}{2} = \frac{1\times2+1}{2} = \frac{3}{2}$

These two fractions are "unlike" fractions. (they have different denominators). Find equivalent fractions with the same denominator. Use this formula: $\frac{a}{b} - \frac{c}{d} = \frac{ad-bc}{bd}$

$\frac{7}{3} - \frac{3}{2} = \frac{(7)(2)-(3)(3)}{3\times2} = \frac{14-9}{6} = \frac{5}{6}$

Example 2. Subtract. $3\frac{4}{7} - 2\frac{3}{4} =$

Solution: Convert mixed numbers into fractions: $3\frac{4}{7} = \frac{3\times7+4}{7} = \frac{25}{7}$ and $2\frac{3}{4} = \frac{2\times4+3}{4} = \frac{11}{4}$

Then: $3\frac{4}{7} - 2\frac{3}{4} = \frac{25}{7} - \frac{11}{4} = \frac{(25)(4)-(11)(7)}{7\times4} = \frac{23}{28}$

Multiplying Mixed Numbers

Use the following steps for multiplying mixed numbers:

- Convert the mixed numbers into fractions. $a\frac{c}{b} = a + \frac{c}{b} = \frac{ab+c}{b}$

- Multiply fractions. $\frac{a}{b} \times \frac{c}{d} = \frac{a \times c}{b \times d}$

- Write your answer in lowest terms.

- If the answer is an improper fraction (numerator is bigger than denominator), convert it into a mixed number.

Examples:

Example 1. Multiply. $4\frac{1}{2} \times 2\frac{2}{5} =$

Solution: Convert mixed numbers into fractions, $4\frac{1}{2} = \frac{4 \times 2 + 1}{2} = \frac{9}{2}$ and
$$2\frac{2}{5} = \frac{2 \times 5 + 2}{5} = \frac{12}{5}$$
Apply the fractions rule for multiplication, $\frac{9}{2} \times \frac{12}{5} = \frac{9 \times 12}{2 \times 5} = \frac{108}{10}$
The answer is an improper fraction. Convert it into a mixed number. $\frac{108}{10} = 10\frac{4}{5}$

Example 2. Multiply. $3\frac{2}{3} \times 2\frac{5}{6} =$

Solution: Converting mixed numbers into fractions, $3\frac{2}{3} \times 2\frac{5}{6} = \frac{11}{3} \times \frac{17}{6}$
Apply the fractions rule for multiplication, $\frac{11}{3} \times \frac{17}{6} = \frac{11 \times 17}{3 \times 6} = \frac{187}{18} = 10\frac{7}{18}$

Example 3. Multiply mixed numbers. $5\frac{1}{4} \times 3\frac{3}{8} =$

Solution: Converting mixed numbers to fractions, $5\frac{1}{4} = \frac{21}{4}$ and $3\frac{3}{8} = \frac{27}{8}$. Multiply

two fractions:

$\frac{21}{4} \times \frac{27}{8} = \frac{21 \times 27}{4 \times 8} = \frac{567}{32} = 17\frac{23}{32}$

bit.ly/3aPy7XJ

Find more at

Dividing Mixed Numbers

Use the following steps for dividing mixed numbers:

- Convert the mixed numbers into fractions. $a\frac{c}{b} = a + \frac{c}{b} = \frac{ab+c}{b}$

- Divide fractions: Keep, Change, Flip: Keep the first fraction, change the division sign to multiplication, and flip the numerator and denominator of the second fraction. Then, solve! $\frac{a}{b} \div \frac{c}{d} = \frac{a}{b} \times \frac{d}{c} = \frac{a \times d}{b \times c}$

- Write your answer in lowest terms.

- If the answer is an improper fraction (numerator is bigger than denominator), convert it into a mixed number.

Examples:

Example 1. Solve. $2\frac{1}{3} \div 1\frac{1}{2}$

Solution: Convert mixed numbers into fractions: $2\frac{1}{3} = \frac{2 \times 3 + 1}{3} = \frac{7}{3}$ and $1\frac{1}{2} = \frac{1 \times 2 + 1}{2} = \frac{3}{2}$
Keep, Change, Flip: $\frac{7}{3} \div \frac{3}{2} = \frac{7}{3} \times \frac{2}{3} = \frac{7 \times 2}{3 \times 3} = \frac{14}{9}$. The answer is an improper fraction.
Convert it into a mixed number: $\frac{14}{9} = 1\frac{5}{9}$

Example 2. Solve. $3\frac{3}{4} \div 2\frac{2}{5}$

Solution: Convert mixed numbers to fractions, then solve:
$3\frac{3}{4} \div 2\frac{2}{5} = \frac{15}{4} \div \frac{12}{5} = \frac{15}{4} \times \frac{5}{12} = \frac{75}{48} = 1\frac{9}{16}$

Example 3. Solve. $2\frac{4}{5} \div 1\frac{2}{3}$

Solution: Converting mixed numbers to fractions: $2\frac{4}{5} \div 1\frac{2}{3} = \frac{14}{5} \div \frac{5}{3}$
Keep, Change, Flip: $\frac{14}{5} \div \frac{5}{3} = \frac{14}{5} \times \frac{3}{5} = \frac{14 \times 3}{5 \times 5} = \frac{42}{25} = 1\frac{17}{25}$

bit.ly/2KLPk9k
Find more at

Chapter 1: Practices

✍ Simplify each fraction.

1) $\frac{2}{8} = \frac{1}{4}$

2) $\frac{5}{15} = \frac{1}{3}$

3) $\frac{10}{90} = \frac{1}{9}$

4) $\frac{12}{16} = \frac{3}{4}$

5) $\frac{25}{45} = \frac{5}{9}$

6) $\frac{42}{54} = \frac{7}{9}$

7) $\frac{48}{60} = \frac{4}{5}$

8) $\frac{52}{169} =$

✍ Find the sum or difference.

9) $\frac{3}{10} + \frac{2}{10} = \frac{5}{10} \quad \frac{1}{2}$

10) $\frac{4}{9} - \frac{1}{9} = \frac{3}{9} \quad \frac{1}{3}$

11) $\frac{2}{3} + \frac{6}{15} = \frac{16}{15} \quad 1\frac{1}{15}$

12) $\frac{17}{24} - \frac{5}{8} = \frac{2}{24} = \frac{1}{12}$

13) $\frac{7}{54} - \frac{1}{69} = \frac{13}{54}$

14) $\frac{4}{5} - \frac{15}{630} = \frac{49}{30}$

15) $\frac{6}{7} - \frac{32}{8} = \frac{27}{56} \quad \frac{35}{36}$

16) $\frac{2}{13} + \frac{1}{4} = \frac{7}{52}$

✍ Find the products or quotients.

17) $\frac{2}{9} \div \frac{4}{3} = \frac{6}{36} = \frac{1}{6}$

18) $\frac{14}{5} \div \frac{28}{35} = 490 \quad 140$

19) $\frac{9}{25} \times \frac{5}{27} = \frac{245}{675} = 15$

20) $\frac{65}{72} \times \frac{12}{15} = 780 \quad \frac{1080}{1080}$

✍ Find the sum.

21) $2\frac{1}{5} + 1\frac{2}{5} =$

22) $5\frac{1}{9} + 2\frac{7}{9} =$

23) $2\frac{3}{4} + 1\frac{1}{8} =$

24) $2\frac{2}{7} + 4\frac{1}{21} =$

25) $5\frac{3}{5} + 1\frac{4}{9} =$

26) $3\frac{3}{11} + 4\frac{6}{7} =$

✎ **Find the difference.**

27) $5\frac{1}{3} - 4\frac{2}{3} =$

28) $4\frac{7}{10} - 1\frac{3}{10} =$

29) $3\frac{1}{3} - 2\frac{2}{9} =$

30) $6\frac{1}{2} - 3\frac{1}{3} =$

31) $4\frac{3}{4} - 2\frac{1}{28} =$

32) $4\frac{2}{7} - 3\frac{1}{6} =$

33) $5\frac{3}{10} - 3\frac{3}{4} =$

34) $6\frac{9}{20} - 2\frac{1}{3} =$

✎ **Find the products.**

35) $1\frac{1}{2} \times 2\frac{3}{7} =$

36) $1\frac{3}{4} \times 1\frac{3}{5} =$

37) $4\frac{1}{2} \times 1\frac{5}{6} =$

38) $1\frac{2}{7} \times 3\frac{1}{5} =$

39) $2\frac{1}{5} \times 5\frac{1}{2} =$

40) $2\frac{1}{2} \times 4\frac{4}{5} =$

41) $3\frac{1}{5} \times 4\frac{1}{2} =$

42) $4\frac{9}{10} \times 4\frac{1}{2} =$

✎ **Solve.**

43) $1\frac{1}{3} \div 1\frac{2}{3} =$

44) $2\frac{1}{4} \div 1\frac{1}{2} =$

45) $5\frac{1}{3} \div 3\frac{1}{2} =$

46) $3\frac{2}{7} \div 1\frac{1}{8} =$

47) $4\frac{1}{5} \div 2\frac{2}{3} =$

48) $1\frac{2}{3} \div 1\frac{3}{8} =$

49) $4\frac{1}{2} \div 2\frac{2}{3} =$

50) $1\frac{2}{11} \div 1\frac{1}{8} =$

Chapter 1: Answers

1) $\frac{1}{4}$

2) $\frac{1}{3}$

3) $\frac{1}{9}$

4) $\frac{3}{4}$

5) $\frac{5}{9}$

6) $\frac{7}{9}$

7) $\frac{4}{5}$

8) $\frac{4}{13}$

9) $\frac{1}{2}$

10) $\frac{1}{3}$

11) $\frac{16}{15} = 1\frac{1}{15}$

12) $\frac{1}{12}$

13) $\frac{1}{54}$

14) $\frac{19}{30}$

15) $\frac{27}{56}$

16) $\frac{21}{52}$

17) $\frac{1}{6}$

18) $\frac{7}{2} = 3\frac{1}{2}$

19) $\frac{1}{15}$

20) $\frac{13}{18}$

21) $3\frac{3}{5}$

22) $7\frac{8}{9}$

23) $3\frac{7}{8}$

24) $6\frac{1}{3}$

25) $7\frac{2}{45}$

26) $8\frac{10}{77}$

27) $\frac{2}{3}$

28) $3\frac{2}{5}$

29) $1\frac{1}{9}$

30) $3\frac{1}{6}$

31) $2\frac{5}{7}$

32) $1\frac{5}{42}$

33) $1\frac{11}{20}$

34) $4\frac{7}{60}$

35) $3\frac{9}{14}$

36) $2\frac{4}{5}$

37) $8\frac{1}{4}$

38) $4\frac{4}{35}$

39) $12\frac{1}{10}$

40) 12

41) $14\frac{2}{5}$

42) $22\frac{1}{20}$

43) $\frac{4}{5}$

44) $1\frac{1}{2}$

45) $1\frac{11}{21}$

46) $2\frac{58}{63}$

47) $1\frac{23}{40}$

48) $1\frac{7}{33}$

49) $1\frac{11}{16}$

50) $1\frac{5}{99}$

CHAPTER

2 Decimals

Math topics that you'll learn in this chapter:

- ☑ Comparing Decimals
- ☑ Rounding Decimals
- ☑ Adding and Subtracting Decimals
- ☑ Multiplying and Dividing Decimals

Comparing Decimals

- A decimal is a fraction written in a special form. For example, instead of writing $\frac{1}{2}$ you can write 0.5

- A Decimal Number contains a Decimal Point. It separates the whole number part from the fractional part of a decimal number.

- Let's review decimal place values: Example: 53.9861

5: tens   3: ones   9: tenths

8: hundredths   6: thousandths   1: tens thousandths

- To compare decimals, compare each digit of two decimals in the same place value. Start from left. Compare hundreds, tens, ones, tenth, hundredth, etc.

- To compare numbers, use these symbols:

Equal to =,   Less than <,   Greater than >

Greater than or equal ≥,   Less than or equal ≤

Examples:

Example 1. Compare 0.03 and 0.30.

Solution: 0.30 *is greater than* 0.03, because the tenth place of 0.30 is 3, but the tenth place of 0.03 is zero. Then: 0.03 < 0.30

Example 2. Compare 0.0217 and 0.217.

Solution: 0.217 *is greater than* 0.0217, because the tenth place of 0.217 is 2, but the tenth place of 0.0217 is zero. Then: 0.0217 < 0.217

Rounding Decimals

- We can round decimals to a certain accuracy or number of decimal places. This is used to make calculations easier to do and results easier to understand when exact values are not too important.

- First, you'll need to remember your place values: For example: 12.4869

  1: tens   2: ones   4: tenths

  8: hundredths   6: thousandths   9: tens thousandths

- To round a decimal, first find the place value you'll round to.

- Find the digit to the right of the place value you're rounding to. If it is 5 or bigger, add 1 to the place value you're rounding to and remove all digits on its right side. If the digit to the right of the place value is less than 5, keep the place value and remove all digits on the right.

Examples:

Example 1. Round 4.3679 to the thousandth place value.

Solution: First, look at the next place value to the right, (tens thousandths). It's 9 and it is greater than 5. Thus add 1 to the digit in the thousandth place. The thousandth place is 7. $\rightarrow 7 + 1 = 8$, then,
The answer is 4.368

Example 2. Round 1.5237 to the nearest hundredth.

Solution: First, look at the digit to the right of hundredth (thousandths place value). It's 3 and it is less than 5, thus remove all the digits to the right of hundredth place. Then, the answer is 1.52

Adding and Subtracting Decimals

- Line up the decimal numbers.

- Add zeros to have the same number of digits for both numbers if necessary.

- Remember your place values: For example: 73.5196

  7: tens   3: ones   5: tenths

  1: hundredths   9: thousandths   6: tens thousandths

- Add or subtract using column addition or subtraction.

Examples:

Example 1. Add. $1.7 + 4.12$

Solution: First, line up the numbers: $\begin{array}{r} 1.7 \\ +\,4.12 \\ \hline \end{array}$ → Add a zero to have the same number of digits for both numbers. $\begin{array}{r} 1.70 \\ +\,4.12 \\ \hline \end{array}$ → Start with the hundredths place: $0 + 2 = 2$, $\begin{array}{r} 1.70 \\ +\,4.12 \\ \hline 2 \end{array}$ → Continue with tenths place: $7 + 1 = 8$, $\begin{array}{r} 1.70 \\ +\,4.12 \\ \hline .82 \end{array}$ → Add the ones place: $4 + 1 = 5$, $\begin{array}{r} 1.70 \\ +\,4.12 \\ \hline 5.82 \end{array}$

Example 2. Find the difference. $5.58 - 4.23$

Solution: First, line up the numbers: $\begin{array}{r} 5.58 \\ -\,4.23 \\ \hline \end{array}$ → Start with the hundredths place: $8 - 3 = 5$, $\begin{array}{r} 5.58 \\ -\,4.23 \\ \hline 5 \end{array}$ → Continue with tenths place. $5 - 2 = 3$, $\begin{array}{r} 5.58 \\ -\,4.23 \\ \hline .35 \end{array}$ → Subtract the ones place. $5 - 4 = 1$, $\begin{array}{r} 5.58 \\ -\,4.23 \\ \hline 1.35 \end{array}$

Multiplying and Dividing Decimals

For multiplying decimals:

- Ignore the decimal point and set up and multiply the numbers as you do with whole numbers.

- Count the total number of decimal places in both of the factors.

- Place the decimal point in the product.

For dividing decimals:

- If the divisor is not a whole number, move the decimal point to the right to make it a whole number. Do the same for the dividend.

- Divide similar to whole numbers.

Examples:

Example 1. Find the product. $0.65 \times 0.24 =$

Solution: Set up and multiply the numbers as you do with whole numbers. Line up the numbers: $\begin{array}{r} 65 \\ \times 24 \\ \hline \end{array}$ → Start with the ones place then continue with other digits

→ $\begin{array}{r} 65 \\ \times 24 \\ \hline 1{,}560 \end{array}$. Count the total number of decimal places in both of the factors. There are four decimals digits. (two for each factor 0.65 and 0.24) Then: $0.65 \times 0.24 = 0.1560$

Example 2. Find the quotient. $1.20 \div 0.4 =$

Solution: The divisor is not a whole number. Multiply it by 10 to get 4: → $0.4 \times 10 = 4$
Do the same for the dividend to get 12. → $1.20 \times 10 = 12$
Now, divide $12 \div 4 = 3$. The answer is 3.

bit.ly/34DZ0cS
Find more at

Chapter 2: Practices

✎ **Compare. Use >, =, and <**

1) 0.5 ☐ 0.6

2) 0.9 ☐ 0.8

3) 0.1 ☐ 0.2

4) 0.02 ☐ 0.06

5) 0.05 ☐ 0.08

6) 0.12 ☐ 0.09

7) 3.2 ☐ 2.5

8) 4.8 ☐ 8.4

9) 0.005 ☐ 0.05

10) 2.02 ☐ 20.020

11) 55.100 ☐ 55.10

12) 0.44 ☐ 0.440

13) 6.01 ☐ 6.0100

14) 0.77 ☐ 77.0

✎ **Round each decimal to the nearest whole number.**

15) 5.8

16) 6.4

17) 12.3

18) 9.2

19) 7.6

20) 22.4

21) 6.8

22) 15.9

23) 13.41

24) 16.78

25) 67.58

26) 42.67

27) 55.89

28) 14.32

29) 78.88

30) 98.29

✎ Find the sum or difference.

31) $12.1 + 36.2 =$

32) $56.3 - 22.2 =$

33) $45.1 + 12.8 =$

34) $27.9 - 16.4 =$

35) $98.8 - 56.6 =$

36) $28.45 + 13.22 =$

37) $16.78 + 45.11 =$

38) $86.16 - 72.12 =$

39) $96.23 - 28.32 =$

40) $57.33 + 67.46 =$

41) $46.26 - 39.49 =$

42) $44.95 + 76.53 =$

43) $79.37 - 52.89 =$

44) $19.99 + 28.7 =$

45) $83.48 - 49.3 =$

46) $19.6 + 42.98 =$

✎ Find the product or quotient.

47) $3.3 \times 0.2 =$

48) $2.4 \div 0.3 =$

49) $8.1 \times 1.4 =$

50) $4.8 \div 0.2 =$

51) $4.1 \times 0.3 =$

52) $8.6 \div 0.2 =$

53) $9.9 \times 0.8 =$

54) $1.84 \div 0.2 =$

55) $2.1 \times 8.4 =$

56) $1.6 \times 4.5 =$

57) $9.2 \times 3.1 =$

58) $36.6 \div 1.6 =$

59) $1.91 \times 5.2 =$

60) $3.65 \times 1.4 =$

61) $24.82 \div 0.4 =$

62) $12.4 \times 4.20 =$

Chapter 2: Answers

1) <
2) >
3) <
4) <
5) <
6) >
7) >
8) <
9) <
10) <
11) =
12) =
13) =
14) <
15) 6
16) 6
17) 12
18) 9
19) 8
20) 22
21) 7

22) 16
23) 13
24) 17
25) 68
26) 43
27) 56
28) 14
29) 79
30) 98
31) 48.3
32) 34.1
33) 57.9
34) 11.5
35) 42.2
36) 41.67
37) 61.89
38) 14.04
39) 67.91
40) 124.79
41) 6.77
42) 121.48

43) 26.48
44) 48.69
45) 34.18
46) 62.58
47) 0.66
48) 8
49) 11.34
50) 24
51) 1.23
52) 43
53) 7.92
54) 9.2
55) 17.64
56) 7.2
57) 28.52
58) 22.875
59) 9.932
60) 5.11
61) 62.05
62) 52.08

CHAPTER

3 Integers and Order of Operations

Math topics that you'll learn in this chapter:

- ☑ Adding and Subtracting Integers
- ☑ Multiplying and Dividing Integers
- ☑ Order of Operations
- ☑ Integers and Absolute Value

Adding and Subtracting Integers

- Integers include zero, counting numbers, and the negative of the counting numbers. $\{\dots, -3, -2, -1, 0, 1, 2, 3, \dots\}$

- Add a positive integer by moving to the right on the number line. (you will get a bigger number)

- Add a negative integer by moving to the left on the number line. (you will get a smaller number)

- Subtract an integer by adding its opposite.

Examples:

Example 1. Solve. $(-2)-(-8) =$

Solution: Keep the first number and convert the sign of the second number to its opposite. (change subtraction into addition. Then: $(-2) + 8 = 6$

Example 2. Solve. $4 + (5 - 10) =$

Solution: First, subtract the numbers in brackets, $5 - 10 = -5$.
Then: $4 + (-5) = \rightarrow$ change addition into subtraction: $4 - 5 = -1$

Example 3. Solve. $(9-14) + 15 =$

Solution: First, subtract the numbers in brackets, $9 - 14 = -5$
Then: $-5 + 15 = \rightarrow -5 + 15 = 10$

Example 4. Solve. $12 + (-3 - 10) =$

Solution: First, subtract the numbers in brackets, $-3 - 10 = -13$
Then: $12 + (-13) = \rightarrow$ change addition into subtraction: $12 - 13 = -1$

Multiplying and Dividing Integers

Use the following rules for multiplying and dividing integers:

- (negative) × (negative) = positive

- (negative) ÷ (negative) = positive

- (negative) × (positive) = negative

- (negative) ÷ (positive) = negative

- (positive) × (positive) = positive

- (positive) ÷ (negative) = negative

Examples:

Example 1. Solve. $3 \times (-4) =$

Solution: Use this rule: (positive) × (negative) = negative.
Then: $(3) \times (-4) = -12$

Example 2. Solve. $(-3) + (-24 \div 3) =$

Solution: First, divide -24 by 3, the numbers in brackets, use this rule:
(negative) ÷ (positive) = negative. Then: $-24 \div 3 = -8$
$(-3) + (-24 \div 3) = (-3) + (-8) = -3 - 8 = -11$

Example 3. Solve. $(12 - 15) \times (-2) =$

Solution: First, subtract the numbers in brackets,
$12 - 15 = -3 \rightarrow (-3) \times (-2) =$
Now use this rule: (negative) × (negative) = positive $\rightarrow (-3) \times (-2) = 6$

Example 4. Solve. $(12 - 8) \div (-4) =$

Solution: First, subtract the numbers in brackets,
$12 - 8 = 4 \rightarrow (4) \div (-4) =$
Now use this rule: (positive) ÷ (negative) = negative $\rightarrow (4) \div (-4) = -1$

bit.ly/3pjQW98

Find more at

Order of Operations

- In Mathematics, "operations" are addition, subtraction, multiplication, division, exponentiation (written as b^n), and grouping.

- When there is more than one math operation in an expression, use PEMDAS: (to memorize this rule, remember the phrase "Please Excuse My Dear Aunt Sally".)

  ❖ Parentheses
  ❖ Exponents
  ❖ Multiplication and Division (from left to right)
  ❖ Addition and Subtraction (from left to right)

Examples:

Example 1. Calculate. $(2 + 6) \div (2^2 \div 4) =$

Solution: First, simplify inside parentheses:
$(8) \div (4 \div 4) = (8) \div (1)$, Then: $(8) \div (1) = 8$

Example 2. Solve. $(6 \times 5) - (14 - 5) =$

Solution: First, calculate within parentheses: $(6 \times 5) - (14 - 5) = (30) - (9)$, Then: $(30) - (9) = 21$

Example 3. Calculate. $-4[(3 \times 6) \div (3^2 \times 2)] =$

Solution: First, calculate within parentheses:
$-4[(18) \div (9 \times 2)] = -4[(18) \div (18)] = -4[1]$
multiply -4 and 1. Then: $-4[1] = -4$

Example 4. Solve. $(28 \div 7) + (-19 + 3) =$

Solution: First, calculate within parentheses:
$(28 \div 7) + (-19 + 3) = (4) + (-16)$ Then: $(4) - (16) = -12$

bit.ly/37LBw7X
Find more at

Integers and Absolute Value

- The absolute value of a number is its distance from zero, in either direction, on the number line. For example, the distance of 9 and -9 from zero on number line is 9.

- The absolute value of an integer is the numerical value without its sign. (negative or positive)

- The vertical bar is used for absolute value as in $|x|$.

- The absolute value of a number is never negative; because it only shows, "how far the number is from zero".

Examples:

Example 1. Calculate. $|14 - 2| \times 5 =$

Solution: First, solve $|14 - 2|$, $\rightarrow |14 - 2| = |12|$, the absolute value of 12 is 12, $|12| = 12$ Then: $12 \times 5 = 60$

Example 2. Solve. $\frac{|-24|}{4} \times |5 - 7| =$

Solution: First, find $|-24|$, $\rightarrow$ the absolute value of -24 is 24,
Then: $|-24| = 24$, $\frac{24}{4} \times |5 - 7| =$
Now, calculate $|5 - 7|$, $\rightarrow |5 - 7| = |-2|$, the absolute value of -2 is 2. $|-2| = 2$
then: $\frac{24}{4} \times 2 = 6 \times 2 = 12$

Example 3. Solve. $|8 - 2| \times \frac{|-4 \times 7|}{2} =$

Solution: First, calculate $|8 - 2|$, $\rightarrow |8 - 2| = |6|$, the absolute value of 6 is 6, $|6| = 6$. Then: $6 \times \frac{|-4 \times 7|}{2}$
Now calculate $|-4 \times 7|$, $\rightarrow |-4 \times 7| = |-28|$, the absolute value of -28 is 28, $|-28| = 28$ Then: $6 \times \frac{28}{2} = 6 \times 14 = 84$

bit.ly/3aD521u
Find more at

Chapter 3: Practices

✍ Find each sum or difference.

1) $-9 + 16 =$

2) $-18 - 6 =$

3) $-24 + 10 =$

4) $30 + (-5) =$

5) $15 + (-3) =$

6) $(-13) + (-4) =$

7) $25 + (3 - 10) =$

8) $12 - (-6 + 9) =$

9) $5 - (-2 + 7) =$

10) $(-11) + (-5 + 6) =$

11) $(-3) + (9 - 16) =$

12) $(-8) - (13 + 4) =$

13) $(-7 + 9) - 39 =$

14) $(-30 + 6) - 14 =$

15) $(-5 + 9) + (-3 + 7) =$

16) $(8 - 19) - (-4 + 12) =$

17) $(-9 + 2) - (6 - 7) =$

18) $(-12 - 5) - (-4 - 14) =$

✍ Solve.

19) $3 \times (-6) =$

20) $(-32) \div 4 =$

21) $(-5) \times 4 =$

22) $(25) \div (-5) =$

23) $(-72) \div 8 =$

24) $(-2) \times (-6) \times 5 =$

25) $(-2) \times 3 \times (-7) =$

26) $(-1) \times (-3) \times (-5) =$

27) $(-2) \times (-3) \times (-6) =$

28) $(-12 + 3) \times (-5) =$

29) $(-3 + 4) \times (-11) =$

30) $(-9) \times (6 - 5) =$

31) $(-3 - 7) \times (-6) =$

32) $(-7 + 3) \times (-9 + 6) =$

33) $(-15) \div (-17 + 12) =$

34) $(-3 - 2) \times (-9 + 7) =$

35) $(-15 + 31) \div (-2) =$

36) $(-64) \div (-16 + 8) =$

✎ Evaluate each expression.

37) $3 + (2 \times 5) =$

38) $(5 \times 4) - 7 =$

39) $(-9 \times 2) + 6 =$

40) $(7 \times 3) - (-5) =$

41) $(-8) + (2 \times 7) =$

42) $(9 - 6) + (3 \times 4) =$

43) $(-19 + 5) + (6 \times 2) =$

44) $(32 \div 4) + (1 - 13) =$

45) $(-36 \div 6) - (12 + 3) =$

46) $(-16 + 5) - (54 \div 9) =$

47) $(-20 + 4) - (35 \div 5) =$

48) $(42 \div 7) + (2 \times 3) =$

49) $(28 \div 4) + (2 \times 6) =$

50) $2[(3 \times 3) - (4 \times 5)] =$

51) $3[(2 \times 8) + (4 \times 3)] =$

52) $2[(9 \times 3) - (6 \times 4)] =$

53) $4[(4 \times 8) \div (4 \times 4)] =$

54) $-5[(10 \times 8) \div (5 \times 8)] =$

✎ Find the answers.

55) $|-5| + |7 - 10| =$

56) $|-4 + 6| + |-2| =$

57) $|-9| + |1 - 9| =$

58) $|-7| - |8 - 12| =$

59) $|9 - 11| + |8 - 15| =$

60) $|-7 + 10| - |-8 + 3| =$

61) $|-12 + 6| - |3 - 9| =$

62) $5 + |2 - 6| + |3 - 4| =$

63) $-4 + |2 - 6| + |1 - 9| =$

64) $|-6| \times |-7| + |2 - 8| =$

65) $|-12| \times |-3| + |4 - 28| =$

66) $|4 \times (-2)| \times |-9| =$

67) $|-3 \times 2| \times |-5| =$

68) $|3 - 12| - |-3 \times 7| =$

69) $|-9| + |-7 \times 5| =$

70) $|-11| + |-6 \times 4| =$

71) $|-4 \times 2 + 6| \times |-2 \times 8| =$

72) $|-1 \times 5 + 2| \times |-4| =$

Chapter 3: Answers

1) 7
2) −24
3) −14
4) 25
5) 12
6) −17
7) 18
8) 9
9) 0
10) −10
11) −10
12) −25
13) −37
14) −38
15) 8
16) −19
17) −6
18) 1
19) −18
20) −8
21) −20
22) −5
23) −9
24) 60

25) 42
26) −15
27) −36
28) 45
29) −11
30) −9
31) 60
32) 12
33) 3
34) 10
35) −8
36) 8
37) 13
38) 13
39) −12
40) 26
41) 6
42) 15
43) −2
44) −4
45) −21
46) −17
47) −23
48) 12

49) 19
50) −22
51) 84
52) 6
53) 8
54) −10
55) 8
56) 4
57) 17
58) 3
59) 9
60) −2
61) 0
62) 10
63) 8
64) 48
65) 60
66) 72
67) 30
68) −12
69) 44
70) 35
71) 32
72) 12

CHAPTER

4 Ratios and Proportions

Math topics that you'll learn in this chapter:

☑ Simplifying Ratios

☑ Proportional Ratios

☑ Similarity and Ratios

Simplifying Ratios

- Ratios are used to make comparisons between two numbers.

- Ratios can be written as a fraction, using the word "to", or with a colon. Example: $\frac{3}{4}$ or "3 to 4" or 3:4

- You can calculate equivalent ratios by multiplying or dividing both sides of the ratio by the same number.

Examples:

Example 1. Simplify. $8:2 =$

Solution: Both numbers 8 and 2 are divisible by 2 , $\Rightarrow 8 \div 2 = 4$, $4 \div 2 = 2$, Then: $8:2 = 4:1$

Example 2. Simplify. $\frac{9}{33} =$

Solution: Both numbers 9 and 33 are divisible by 3, $\Rightarrow 33 \div 3 = 11$, $9 \div 3 = 3$, Then: $\frac{9}{33} = \frac{3}{11}$

Example 3. There are 24 students in a class and 10 are girls. Write the ratio of girls to boys.

Solution: Subtract 10 from 24 to find the number of boys in the class. $24 - 10 = 14$. There are 14 boys in the class. So, the ratio of girls to boys is $10:14$. Now, simplify this ratio. Both 14 and 10 are divisible by 2. Then: $14 \div 2 = 7$, and $10 \div 2 = 5$. In the simplest form, this ratio is $5:7$

Example 4. A recipe calls for butter and sugar in the ratio $3:4$. If you're using 9 cups of butter, how many cups of sugar should you use?

Solution: Since you use 9 cups of butter, or 3 times as much, you need to multiply the amount of sugar by 3. Then: $4 \times 3 = 12$. So, you need to use 12 cups of sugar. You can solve this using equivalent fractions: $\frac{3}{4} = \frac{9}{12}$

bit.ly/3nKwq0Z
Find more at

Proportional Ratios

- Two ratios are proportional if they represent the same relationship.

- A proportion means that two ratios are equal. It can be written in two ways: $\frac{a}{b} = \frac{c}{d}$ $\qquad a : b = c : d$

- The proportion $\frac{a}{b} = \frac{c}{d}$ can be written as: $a \times d = c \times b$

Examples:

Example 1. Solve this proportion for x. $\qquad \frac{2}{5} = \frac{6}{x}$

Solution: Use cross multiplication: $\frac{2}{5} = \frac{6}{x} \Rightarrow 2 \times x = 6 \times 5 \Rightarrow 2x = 30$

Divide both sides by 2 to find x: $\quad x = \frac{30}{2} \Rightarrow x = 15$

Example 2. If a box contains red and blue balls in ratio of $3 : 5$ red to blue, how many red balls are there if 45 blue balls are in the box?

Solution: Write a proportion and solve. $\frac{3}{5} = \frac{x}{45}$

Use cross multiplication: $3 \times 45 = 5 \times x \Rightarrow 135 = 5x$

Divide to find x: $\quad x = \frac{135}{5} \Rightarrow x = 27$. There are 27 red balls in the box.

Example 3. Solve this proportion for x. $\qquad \frac{4}{9} = \frac{16}{x}$

Solution: Use cross multiplication: $\quad \frac{4}{9} = \frac{16}{x} \Rightarrow 4 \times x = 9 \times 16 \Rightarrow 4x = 144$

Divide to find x: $\quad x = \frac{144}{4} \Rightarrow x = 36$

Example 4. Solve this proportion for x. $\frac{5}{7} = \frac{20}{x}$

Solution: Use cross multiplication: $\quad \frac{5}{7} = \frac{20}{x} \Rightarrow 5 \times x = 7 \times 20 \Rightarrow 5x = 140$

Divide to find x: $\quad x = \frac{140}{5} \Rightarrow x = 28$

Similarity and Ratios

- Two figures are similar if they have the same shape.

- Two or more figures are similar if the corresponding angles are equal, and the corresponding sides are in proportion.

Examples:

Example 1. The following triangles are similar. What is the value of the unknown side?

Example 2.

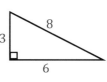

Solution: Find the corresponding sides and write a proportion.
$\frac{8}{16} = \frac{6}{x}$. Now, use the cross product to solve for x:

$\frac{8}{16} = \frac{6}{x} \rightarrow 8 \times x = 16 \times 6 \rightarrow 8x = 96$. Divide both sides by 8. Then: $8x = 96 \rightarrow x = \frac{96}{8} \rightarrow x = 12$

The missing side is 12.

Example 3. Two rectangles are similar. The first is 5 feet wide and 15 feet long. The second is 10 feet wide. What is the length of the second rectangle?

Solution: Let's put x for the length of the second rectangle. Since two rectangles are similar, their corresponding sides are in proportion. Write a proportion and solve for the missing number.

$\frac{5}{10} = \frac{15}{x} \rightarrow 5x = 10 \times 15 \rightarrow 5x = 150 \rightarrow x = \frac{150}{5} = 30$

The length of the second rectangle is 30 feet.

Chapter 4: Practices

✎ Reduce each ratio.

1) $2:18 = $ ___ : ___

2) $5:35 = $ ___ : ___

3) $8:72 = $ ___ : __

4) $24:36 = $ ___ : ___

5) $25:40 = $ ___ : ___

6) $40:72 = $ ___ : ___

7) $28:63 = $ ___ : ___

8) $18:81 = $ ___ : ___

9) $13:52 = $ ___ : ___

10) $56:72 = $ ___ : ___

11) $42:63 = $ ___ : ___

12) $32:96 = $ ___ : ___

✎ Solve.

13) Bob has 16 red cards and 20 green cards. What is the ratio of Bob's red cards to his green cards? _____

14) In a party, 34 soft drinks are required for every 20 guests. If there are 260 guests, how many soft drinks are required? _____

15) Sara has 56 blue pens and 28 black pens. What is the ratio of Sara's black pens to her blue pens? _____

16) In Jack's class, 48 of the students are tall and 20 are short. In Michael's class 28 students are tall and 12 students are short. Which class has a higher ratio of tall to short students? _____

17) The price of 6 apples at the Quick Market is $1.52. The price of 5 of the same apples at Walmart is $1.32. Which place is the better buy? _____

18) The bakers at a Bakery can make 180 bagels in 6 hours. How many bagels can they bake in 16 hours? What is that rate per hour? _____

19) You can buy 6 cans of green beans at a supermarket for $3.48. How much does it cost to buy 38 cans of green beans? _____

✍ Solve each proportion.

20) $\frac{3}{2} = \frac{9}{x} \Rightarrow x = $ ____

21) $\frac{7}{2} = \frac{x}{4} \Rightarrow x = $ ____

22) $\frac{1}{3} = \frac{2}{x} \Rightarrow x = $ ____

23) $\frac{1}{4} = \frac{5}{x} \Rightarrow x = $ ____

24) $\frac{9}{6} = \frac{x}{2} \Rightarrow x = $ ____

25) $\frac{3}{6} = \frac{5}{x} \Rightarrow x = $ ____

26) $\frac{7}{x} = \frac{2}{6} \Rightarrow x = $ ____

27) $\frac{2}{x} = \frac{4}{10} \Rightarrow x = $ ____

28) $\frac{3}{2} = \frac{x}{8} \Rightarrow x = $ ____

29) $\frac{x}{6} = \frac{5}{3} \Rightarrow x = $ ____

30) $\frac{3}{9} = \frac{5}{x} \Rightarrow x = $ ____

31) $\frac{4}{18} = \frac{2}{x} \Rightarrow x = $ ____

32) $\frac{6}{16} = \frac{3}{x} \Rightarrow x = $ ____

33) $\frac{2}{5} = \frac{x}{20} \Rightarrow x = $ ____

34) $\frac{28}{8} = \frac{x}{2} \Rightarrow x = $ ____

35) $\frac{3}{5} = \frac{x}{15} \Rightarrow x = $ ____

36) $\frac{2}{7} = \frac{x}{14} \Rightarrow x = $ ____

37) $\frac{x}{18} = \frac{3}{2} \Rightarrow x = $ ____

38) $\frac{x}{24} = \frac{2}{6} \Rightarrow x = $ ____

39) $\frac{5}{x} = \frac{4}{20} \Rightarrow x = $ ____

40) $\frac{10}{x} = \frac{20}{80} \Rightarrow x = $ ____

41) $\frac{90}{6} = \frac{x}{2} \Rightarrow x = $ ____

✍ Solve each problem.

42) Two rectangles are similar. The first is 8 *feet* wide and 32 *feet* long. The second is 12 *feet* wide. What is the length of the second rectangle?

_____

43) Two rectangles are similar. One is 4.6 *meters* by 7 *meters*. The longer side of the second rectangle is 28 *meters*. What is the other side of the second rectangle? _____

Chapter 4: Answers

1) $1:9$
2) $1:7$
3) $1:9$
4) $2:3$
5) $5:8$
6) $5:9$
7) $4:9$
8) $2:9$

9) $1:4$
10) $7:9$
11) $2:3$
12) $1:3$
13) $4:5$
14) 442
15) $1:2$

16) *Jack's class*: $\frac{48}{20} = \frac{12}{5}$ *Michael's class*: $\frac{28}{12} = \frac{7}{3}$ Jack's class has a higher ratio of tall to short student: $\frac{12}{5} > \frac{7}{3}$

17) Quick market
18) 480, 30 bagels per hour
19) $22.04
20) 6
21) 14
22) 6
23) 20
24) 3
25) 10
26) 21
27) 5
28) 12
29) 10
30) 15

31) 9
32) 8
33) 8
34) 7
35) 9
36) 4
37) 27
38) 8
39) 25
40) 40
41) 30
42) 48 *feet*
43) 18.4 *meters*

CHAPTER

5 Percentage

Math topics that you'll learn in this chapter:

- ☑ Percent Problems
- ☑ Percent of Increase and Decrease
- ☑ Discount, Tax and Tip
- ☑ Simple Interest

Percent Problems

- Percent is a ratio of a number and 100. It always has the same denominator, 100. The percent symbol is "%".

- Percent means "per 100". So, 20% is 20/100.

- In each percent problem, we are looking for the base, or part or the percent.

- Use these equations to find each missing section in a percent problem:

    ❖ Base = Part ÷ Percent

    ❖ Part = Percent × Base

    ❖ Percent = Part ÷ Base

Examples:

Example 1. What is 20% of 40?

Solution: In this problem, we have percent (20%) and base (40) and we are looking for the "part". Use this formula: $part = percent \times base$.

Then: $part = 20\% \times 40 = \frac{20}{100} \times 40 = 0.20 \times 40 = 8$. The answer: 20% of 40 is 8.

Example 2. 25 is what percent of 500?

Solution: In this problem, we are looking for the percent. Use this equation: $Percent = Part \div Base \rightarrow Percent = 25 \div 500 = 0.05 = 5\%$.

Then: 25 is 5 percent of 500.

Percent of Increase and Decrease

- Percent of change (increase or decrease) is a mathematical concept that represents the degree of change over time.

- To find the percentage of increase or decrease:

  1. New Number – Original Number

  2. The result ÷ Original Number × 100

- Or use this formula: Percent of change = $\frac{new\ number - original\ number}{original\ number} \times 100$

- Note: If your answer is a negative number, then this is a percentage decrease. If it is positive, then this is a percentage increase.

Examples:

Example 1. The price of a shirt increases from \$30 to \$40. What is the percentage increase?

Solution: First, find the difference: $40 - 30 = 10$

Then: $10 \div 30 \times 100 = \frac{10}{30} \times 100 = 33.33$. The percentage increase is 33.33. It means that the price of the shirt increased by 33.33%.

Example 2. The price of a table increased from \$20 to \$50. What is the percent of increase?

Solution: Use percentage formula:

$Percent\ of\ change = \dfrac{new\ number - original\ number}{original\ number} \times 100 =$

$\frac{50-20}{20} \times 100 = \frac{30}{20} \times 100 = 1.5 \times 100 = 150$. The percentage increase is 150. It means that the price of the table increased by 150%.

bit.ly/3pgPQes
Find more at

Discount, Tax and Tip

- To find the discount: Multiply the regular price by the rate of discount

- To find the selling price: Original price – discount

- To find tax: Multiply the tax rate to the taxable amount (income, property value, etc.)

- To find the tip, multiply the rate to the selling price.

Examples:

Example 1. With an 20% discount, Ella saved $50 on a dress. What was the original price of the dress?

Solution: let x be the original price of the dress. Then: 20 % *of* $x = 50$. Write an equation and solve for x: $0.20 \times x = 50 \rightarrow x = \frac{50}{0.20} = 250$. The original price of the dress was $250.

Example 2. Sophia purchased a new computer for a price of $820 at the Apple Store. What is the total amount her credit card is charged if the sales tax is 5%?

Solution: The taxable amount is $820, and the tax rate is 5%. Then: $Tax = 0.05 \times 820 = 41$

Final price = Selling price + Tax → final price = $820 + $41 = $861

Example 3. Nicole and her friends went out to eat at a restaurant. If their bill was $60.00 and they gave their server a 15% tip, how much did they pay altogether?

Solution: First, find the tip. To find the tip, multiply the rate to the bill amount. $Tip = 60 \times 0.15 = 9$. The final price is: $60 + $9 = $69

Simple Interest

- Simple Interest: The charge for borrowing money or the return for lending it.

- Simple interest is calculated on the initial amount (principal).

- To solve a simple interest problem, use this formula:

Interest = principal × rate × time $(I = p \times r \times t = prt)$

Examples:

Example 1. Find simple interest for $200 investment at 5% for 3 years.

Solution: Use Interest formula:
$I = prt$ $(P = \$200, r = 5\% = \frac{5}{100} = 0.05$ and $t = 3)$
Then: $I = 200 \times 0.05 \times 3 = \$30$

Example 2. Find simple interest for $1,200 at 8% for 6 years.

Solution: Use Interest formula:
$I = prt$ $(P = \$1,200, r = 8\% = \frac{8}{100} = 0.08$ and $t = 6)$
Then: $I = 1,200 \times 0.08 \times 6 = \$576$

Example 3. Andy received a student loan to pay for his educational expenses this year. What is the interest on the loan if he borrowed $4,500 at 6% for 5 years?

Solution: Use Interest formula: $I = prt$. $P = \$4,500, r = 6\% = 0.06$ and $t = 5$
Then: $I = 4,500 \times 0.06 \times 5 = \$1,350$

Example 4. Bob is starting his own small business. He borrowed $20,000 from the bank at a 8% rate for 6 months. Find the interest Bob will pay on this loan.

Solution: Use Interest formula:
$I = prt$. $P = \$20,000, r = 8\% = 0.08$ and $t = 0.5$ (6 months is half year). Then: $I = 20,000 \times 0.08 \times 0.5 = \$800$

Chapter 5: Practices

✎ Solve each problem.

1) What is 15% of 60? ____

2) What is 55% of 800? ____

3) What is 22% of 120? ____

4) What is 18% of 40? ____

5) 90 is what percent of 200? ____%

6) 30 is what percent of 150? ____%

7) 14 is what percent of 250? ____%

8) 60 is what percent of 300? ____%

9) 30 is 120 percent of what number? ____

10) 120 is 20 percent of what number? ____

11) 15 is 5 percent of what number? ____

12) 22 is 20% of what number? ____

✎ Solve each problem.

13) Bob got a raise, and his hourly wage increased from $15 to $21. What is the percent increase? _____ %

14) The price of a pair of shoes increases from $32 to $36. What is the percent increase? ___ %

15) At a Coffee Shop, the price of a cup of coffee increased from $1.35 to $1.62. What is the percent increase in the cost of the coffee? _____ %

16) A $45 shirt now selling for $36 is discounted by what percent? _____ %

17) Joe scored 30 out of 35 marks in Algebra, 20 out of 30 marks in science and 58 out of 70 marks in mathematics. In which subject his percentage of marks is best? _____

18) Emma purchased a computer for $420. The computer is regularly priced at $480. What was the percent discount Emma received on the computer? _____

19) A chemical solution contains 15% alcohol. If there is 54 ml of alcohol, what is the volume of the solution? _____

✍ Find the selling price of each item.

20) Original price of a computer: $600

    Tax: 8%, Selling price: $_____

21) Original price of a laptop: $450

    Tax: 10%, Selling price: $_____

22) Nicolas hired a moving company. The company charged $500 for its services, and Nicolas gives the movers a 14% tip. How much does Nicolas tip the movers? $_____

23) Mason has lunch at a restaurant and the cost of his meal is $40. Mason wants to leave a 20% tip. What is Mason's total bill, including tip? $_____

✍ Determine the simple interest for the following loans.

24) $1,000 *at 5% for 4 years.* $__

25) $400 *at 3% for 5 years.* $__

26) $240 *at 4% for 3 years.* $__

27) $500 at 4.5% for 6 years. $__

✍ Solve.

28) A new car, valued at $20,000, depreciates at 8% per year. What is the value of the car one year after purchase? $_____

29) Sara puts $7,000 into an investment yielding 3% annual simple interest; she left the money in for five years. How much interest does Sara get at the end of those five years? $_____

Chapter 5: Answers

1) 9

2) 440

3) 26.4

4) 7.2

5) 45%

6) 20%

7) 5.6%

8) 20%

9) 25

10) 600

11) 300

12) 110

13) 40%

14) 12.5%

15) 20%

16) 20%

17) Algebra

18) 12.5%

19) 360 ml

20) $648.00

21) $495.00

22) $70.00

23) $48.00

24) $200.00

25) $60.00

26) $28.80

27) $135.00

28) $18.400

29) $1,050

CHAPTER

6 Exponents and Variables

Math topics that you'll learn in this chapter:

- ☑ Multiplication Property of Exponents
- ☑ Division Property of Exponents
- ☑ Powers of Products and Quotients
- ☑ Zero and Negative Exponents
- ☑ Negative Exponents and Negative Bases
- ☑ Scientific Notation
- ☑ Radicals

Multiplication Property of Exponents

- Exponents are shorthand for repeated multiplication of the same number by itself. For example, instead of 2×2, we can write 2^2. For $3 \times 3 \times 3 \times 3$, we can write 3^4

- In algebra, a variable is a letter used to stand for a number. The most common letters are: $x, y, z, a, b, c, m,$ and n.

- Exponent's rules: $x^a \times x^b = x^{a+b}$, $\dfrac{x^a}{x^b} = x^{a-b}$

$$(x^a)^b = x^{a \times b} \qquad\qquad (xy)^a = x^a \times y^a \qquad\qquad \left(\dfrac{a}{b}\right)^c = \dfrac{a^c}{b^c}$$

Examples:

Example 1. Multiply. $2x^2 \times 3x^4$

Solution: Use Exponent's rules: $x^a \times x^b = x^{a+b} \rightarrow x^2 \times x^4 = x^{2+4} = x^6$
Then: $2x^2 \times 3x^4 = 6x^6$

Example 2. Simplify. $(x^4 y^2)^2$

Solution: Use Exponent's rules: $(x^a)^b = x^{a \times b}$.
Then: $(x^4 y^2)^2 = x^{4 \times 2} y^{2 \times 2} = x^8 y^4$

Example 3. Multiply. $5x^8 \times 6x^5$

Solution: Use Exponent's rules: $x^a \times x^b = x^{a+b} \rightarrow x^8 \times x^5 = x^{8+5} = x^{13}$
Then: $5x^8 \times 6x^5 = 30x^{13}$

Example 4. Simplify. $(x^4 y^7)^3$

Solution: Use Exponent's rules: $(x^a)^b = x^{a \times b}$.
Then: $(x^4 y^7)^3 = x^{4 \times 3} y^{7 \times 3} = x^{12} y^{21}$

Division Property of Exponents

- Exponents are shorthand for repeated multiplication of the same number by itself. For example, instead of 3×3, we can write 3^2. For $2 \times 2 \times 2$, we can write 2^3

- For division of exponents use following formulas:

$$\frac{x^a}{x^b} = x^{a-b} \ , x \neq 0, \ \frac{x^a}{x^b} = \frac{1}{x^{b-a}} \ , x \neq 0, \qquad \frac{1}{x^b} = x^{-b}$$

Examples:

Example 1. Simplify. $\frac{16x^3y}{2xy^2} =$

Solution: First, cancel the common factor: $2 \rightarrow \frac{16x^3y}{2xy^2} = \frac{8x^3y}{xy^2}$

Use Exponent's rules: $\frac{x^a}{x^b} = x^{a-b} \ \rightarrow \frac{x^3}{x} = x^{3-1} = x^2$ and $\frac{y}{y^2} = \frac{1}{y^{2-1}} = \frac{1}{y}$

Then: $\frac{16x^3y}{2xy^2} = \frac{8x^2}{y}$

Example 2. Simplify. $\frac{24x^8}{3x^6} =$

Solution: Use Exponent's rules: $\frac{x^a}{x^b} = x^{b-a} \ \rightarrow \frac{x^8}{x^6} = x^{8-6} = x^2$

Then: $\frac{24x^8}{3x^6} = 8x^2$

Example 3. Simplify. $\frac{7x^4y^2}{28x^3y} =$

Solution: First, cancel the common factor: $7 \rightarrow \frac{x^4y^2}{4x^3y}$

Use Exponent's rules: $\frac{x^a}{x^b} = x^{a-b} \ \rightarrow \frac{x^4}{x^3} = x^{4-3} = x$ and $\frac{y^2}{y} = y$

Then: $\frac{7x^4y^2}{28x^3y} = \frac{xy}{4}$

Powers of Products and Quotients

- Exponents are shorthand for repeated multiplication of the same number by itself. For example, instead of $2 \times 2 \times 2$, we can write 2^3. For $3 \times 3 \times 3 \times 3$, we can write 3^4

- For any nonzero numbers a and b and any integer x, $(ab)^x = a^x \times b^x$ and $\left(\frac{a}{b}\right)^c = \frac{a^c}{b^c}$

Examples:

Example 1. Simplify. $(3x^3y^2)^2$

Solution: Use Exponent's rules: $(x^a)^b = x^{a \times b}$
$(3x^3y^2)^2 = (3)^2(x^3)^2(y^2)^2 = 9x^{3\times2}y^{2\times2} = 9x^6y^4$

Example 2. Simplify. $\left(\frac{2x^3}{3x^2}\right)^2$

Solution: First, cancel the common factor: $x \rightarrow \left(\frac{2x^3}{3x^2}\right) = \left(\frac{2x}{3}\right)^2$
Use Exponent's rules: $\left(\frac{a}{b}\right)^c = \frac{a^c}{b^c}$, Then: $\left(\frac{2x}{3}\right)^2 = \frac{(2x)^2}{(3)^2} = \frac{4x^2}{9}$

Example 3. Simplify. $\left(-4x^3y^5\right)^2$

Solution: Use Exponent's rules: $(x^a)^b = x^{a \times b}$
$$\left(-4x^3y^5\right)^2 = (-4)^2(x^3)^2\left(y^5\right)^2 = 16x^{3\times2}y^{5\times2} = 16x^6y^{10}$$

Example 4. Simplify. $\left(\frac{5x}{4x^2}\right)^2$

Solution: First, cancel the common factor: $x \rightarrow \left(\frac{5x}{4x^2}\right)^2 = \left(\frac{5}{4x}\right)^2$
Use Exponent's rules: $\left(\frac{a}{b}\right)^c = \frac{a^c}{b^c}$, Then: $\left(\frac{5}{4x}\right)^2 = \frac{5^2}{(4x)^2} = \frac{25}{16x^2}$

Zero and Negative Exponents

- Zero-Exponent Rule: $a^0 = 1$, this means that anything raised to the zero power is 1. For example: $(5xy)^0 = 1$

- A negative exponent simply means that the base is on the wrong side of the fraction line, so you need to flip the base to the other side. For instance, "x^{-2}" (pronounced as "ecks to the minus two") just means "x^2" but underneath, as in $\frac{1}{x^2}$.

Examples:

Example 1. Evaluate. $\left(\frac{4}{5}\right)^{-2} =$

Solution: Use negative exponent's rule: $\left(\frac{x^a}{x^b}\right)^{-2} = \left(\frac{x^b}{x^a}\right)^2 \rightarrow \left(\frac{4}{5}\right)^{-2} = \left(\frac{5}{4}\right)^2 =$
Then: $\left(\frac{5}{4}\right)^2 = \frac{5^2}{4^2} = \frac{25}{16}$

Example 2. Evaluate. $\left(\frac{3}{2}\right)^{-3} =$

Solution: Use negative exponent's rule: $\left(\frac{x^a}{x^b}\right)^{-3} = \left(\frac{x^b}{x^a}\right)^3 \rightarrow \left(\frac{3}{2}\right)^{-3} = \left(\frac{2}{3}\right)^3 =$
Then: $\left(\frac{2}{3}\right)^3 = \frac{2^3}{3^3} = \frac{8}{27}$

Example 3. Evaluate. $\left(\frac{a}{b}\right)^0 =$

Solution: Use zero-exponent Rule: $a^0 = 1$
Then: $\left(\frac{a}{b}\right)^0 = 1$

Example 4. Evaluate. $\left(\frac{4}{7}\right)^{-1} =$

Solution: Use negative exponent's rule: $\left(\frac{x^a}{x^b}\right)^{-1} = \left(\frac{x^b}{x^a}\right)^1 \rightarrow \left(\frac{4}{7}\right)^{-1} = \left(\frac{7}{4}\right)^1 = \frac{7}{4}$

bit.ly/3rnkh4v
Find more at

Negative Exponents and Negative Bases

- A negative exponent is the reciprocal of that number with a positive exponent. $(3)^{-2} = \frac{1}{3^2}$

- To simplify a negative exponent, make the power positive!

- The parenthesis is important! -5^{-2} is not the same as $(-5)^{-2}$

$$-5^{-2} = -\frac{1}{5^2} \text{ and } (-5)^{-2} = +\frac{1}{5^2}$$

Examples:

Example 1. Simplify. $\left(\frac{2a}{3c}\right)^{-2} =$

Solution: Use negative exponent's rule: $\left(\frac{x^a}{x^b}\right)^{-2} = \left(\frac{x^b}{x^a}\right)^2 \rightarrow \left(\frac{2a}{3c}\right)^{-2} = \left(\frac{3c}{2a}\right)^2$

Now use exponent's rule: $\left(\frac{a}{b}\right)^c = \frac{a^c}{b^c} \rightarrow = \left(\frac{3c}{2a}\right)^2 = \frac{3^2 c^2}{2^2 a^2}$

Then: $\frac{3^2 c^2}{2^2 a^2} = \frac{9c^2}{4a^2}$

Example 2. Simplify. $\left(\frac{x}{4y}\right)^{-3} =$

Solution: Use negative exponent's rule: $\left(\frac{x^a}{x^b}\right)^{-3} = \left(\frac{x^b}{x^a}\right)^3 \rightarrow \left(\frac{x}{4y}\right)^{-3} = \left(\frac{4y}{x}\right)^3$

Now use exponent's rule: $\left(\frac{a}{b}\right)^c = \frac{a^c}{b^c} \rightarrow \left(\frac{4y}{x}\right)^3 = \frac{4^3 y^3}{x^3} = \frac{64y^3}{x^3}$

Example 3. Simplify. $\left(\frac{5a}{2c}\right)^{-2} =$

Solution: Use negative exponent's rule: $\left(\frac{x^a}{x^b}\right)^{-2} = \left(\frac{x^b}{x^a}\right)^2 \rightarrow \left(\frac{5a}{2c}\right)^{-2} = \left(\frac{2c}{5a}\right)^2$

Now use exponent's rule: $\left(\frac{a}{b}\right)^c = \frac{a^c}{b^c} \rightarrow = \left(\frac{2c}{5a}\right)^2 = \frac{2^2 c^2}{5^2 a^2}$

Then: $\frac{2^2 c^2}{5^2 a^2} = \frac{4c^2}{25a^2}$

Scientific Notation

- Scientific notation is used to write very big or very small numbers in decimal form.

- In scientific notation, all numbers are written in the form of: $m \times 10^n$, where m is greater than 1 and less than 10.

- To convert a number from scientific notation to standard form, move the decimal point to the left (if the exponent of ten is a negative number), or to the right (if the exponent is positive).

Examples:

Example 1. Write 0.00024 in scientific notation.

Solution: First, move the decimal point to the right so you have a number between 1 and 10. That number is 2.4. Now, determine how many places the decimal moved in step 1 by the power of 10. We moved the decimal point 4 digits to the right. Then: $10^{-4} \rightarrow$ When the decimal moved to the right, the exponent is negative. Then: $0.00024 = 2.4 \times 10^{-4}$

Example 2. Write 3.8×10^{-5} in standard notation.

Solution: $10^{-5} \rightarrow$ When the decimal moved to the right, the exponent is negative. Then: $3.8 \times 10^{-5} = 0.000038$

Example 3. Write 0.00031 in scientific notation.

Solution: First, move the decimal point to the right so you have a number between 1 and 10. Then: $m = 3.1$, Now, determine how many places the decimal moved in step 1 by the power of 10.
$10^{-4} \rightarrow$ Then: $0.00031 = 3.1 \times 10^{-4}$

Example 4. Write 6.2×10^5 in standard notation.

Solution: $10^5 \rightarrow$ The exponent is positive 5. Then, move the decimal point to the right five digits. (remember $6.2 = 6.20000$),
Then: $6.2 \times 10^5 = 620000$

bit.ly/3nOwJYP
Find more at

Radicals

- If n is a positive integer and x is a real number, then: $\sqrt[n]{x} = x^{\frac{1}{n}}$,

$$\sqrt[n]{xy} = x^{\frac{1}{n}} \times y^{\frac{1}{n}}, \ \sqrt[n]{\frac{x}{y}} = \frac{x^{\frac{1}{n}}}{y^{\frac{1}{n}}}, \text{ and } \sqrt[n]{x} \times \sqrt[n]{y} = \sqrt[n]{xy}$$

- A square root of x is a number r whose square is: $r^2 = x$ (r is a square root of x)

- To add and subtract radicals, we need to have the same values under the radical. For example: $\sqrt{3} + \sqrt{3} = 2\sqrt{3}$, $3\sqrt{5} - \sqrt{5} = 2\sqrt{5}$

Examples:

Example 1. Find the square root of $\sqrt{121}$.

Solution: First, factor the number: $121 = 11^2$, Then: $\sqrt{121} = \sqrt{11^2}$,
Now use radical rule: $\sqrt[n]{a^n} = a$. Then: $\sqrt{121} = \sqrt{11^2} = 11$

Example 2. Evaluate. $\sqrt{4} \times \sqrt{16} =$

Solution: Find the values of $\sqrt{4}$ and $\sqrt{16}$. Then: $\sqrt{4} \times \sqrt{16} = 2 \times 4 = 8$

Example 3. Solve. $5\sqrt{2} + 9\sqrt{2}$.

Solution: Since we have the same values under the radical, we can add these two radicals: $5\sqrt{2} + 9\sqrt{2} = 14\sqrt{2}$

Example 4. Evaluate. $\sqrt{2} \times \sqrt{50} =$

Solution: Use this radical rule: $\sqrt[n]{x} \times \sqrt[n]{y} = \sqrt[n]{xy} \rightarrow \sqrt{2} \times \sqrt{50} = \sqrt{100}$
The square root of 100 is 10. Then: $\sqrt{2} \times \sqrt{50} = \sqrt{100} = 10$

Chapter 6: Practices

✍ Find the products.

1) $x^2 \times 4xy^2 =$

2) $3x^2y \times 5x^3y^2 =$

3) $6x^4y^2 \times x^2y^3 =$

4) $7xy^3 \times 2x^2y =$

5) $-5x^5y^5 \times x^3y^2 =$

6) $-8x^3y^2 \times 3x^3y^2 =$

7) $-6x^2y^6 \times 5x^4y^2 =$

8) $-3x^3y^3 \times 2x^3y^2 =$

9) $-6x^5y^3 \times 4x^4y^3 =$

10) $-2x^4y^3 \times 5x^6y^2 =$

11) $-7y^6 \times 3x^6y^3 =$

12) $-9x^4 \times 2x^4y^2 =$

✍ Simplify.

13) $\frac{5^3 \times 5^4}{5^9 \times 5} =$

14) $\frac{3^3 \times 3^2}{7^2 \times 7} =$

15) $\frac{15x^5}{5x^3} =$

16) $\frac{16x^3}{4x^5} =$

17) $\frac{72y^2}{8x^3y^6} =$

18) $\frac{10x^3y^4}{50x^2y^3} =$

19) $\frac{13y^2}{52x^4y^4} =$

20) $\frac{50xy^3}{200x^3y^4} =$

21) $\frac{48x^2}{56x^2y^2} =$

22) $\frac{81y^6x}{54x^4y^3} =$

✍ Solve.

23) $(x^3y^3)^2 =$

24) $(3x^3y^4)^3 =$

25) $(4x \times 6xy^3)^2 =$

26) $(5x \times 2y^3)^3 =$

27) $\left(\frac{9x}{x^3}\right)^2 =$

28) $\left(\frac{3y}{18y^2}\right)^2 =$

29) $\left(\frac{3x^2y^3}{24x^4y^2}\right)^3 =$

30) $\left(\frac{26x^5y^3}{52x^3y^5}\right)^2 =$

31) $\left(\frac{18x^7y^4}{72x^5y^2}\right)^2 =$

32) $\left(\frac{12x^6y^4}{48x^5y^3}\right)^2 =$

Evaluate each expression. (Zero and Negative Exponents)

33) $\left(\frac{1}{4}\right)^{-2} =$

34) $\left(\frac{1}{3}\right)^{-2} =$

35) $\left(\frac{1}{7}\right)^{-3} =$

36) $\left(\frac{2}{5}\right)^{-3} =$

37) $\left(\frac{2}{3}\right)^{-3} =$

38) $\left(\frac{3}{5}\right)^{-4} =$

Write each expression with positive exponents.

39) $x^{-7} =$

40) $3y^{-5} =$

41) $15y^{-3} =$

42) $-20x^{-4} =$

43) $12a^{-3}b^5 =$

44) $25a^3b^{-4}c^{-3} =$

45) $-4x^5y^{-3}z^{-6} =$

46) $\frac{18y}{x^3y^{-2}} =$

47) $\frac{20a^{-2}b}{-12c^{-4}}$

Write each number in scientific notation.

48) $0.00412 =$

49) $0.000053 =$

50) $66,000 =$

51) $72,000,000 =$

Evaluate.

52) $\sqrt{8} \times \sqrt{8} =$ ....

53) $\sqrt{36} - \sqrt{9} =$ ....

54) $\sqrt{81} + \sqrt{16} =$ ....

55) $\sqrt{4} \times \sqrt{25} =$ ....

56) $\sqrt{2} \times \sqrt{32} =$ ....

57) $4\sqrt{3} + 5\sqrt{3} =$ ....

Chapter 6: Answers

1) $4x^3y^2$
2) $15x^5y^3$
3) $6x^6y^5$
4) $14x^3y^4$
5) $-5x^8y^7$
6) $-24x^6y^4$
7) $-30x^6y^8$
8) $-6x^6y^5$
9) $-24x^9y^6$
10) $-10x^{10}y^5$
11) $-21x^6y^9$
12) $-18x^8y^2$
13) $\frac{1}{125}$
14) $\frac{243}{343}$
15) $3x^2$
16) $\frac{4}{x^2}$
17) $\frac{9}{x^3y^4}$
18) $\frac{xy}{5}$
19) $\frac{1}{4x^4y^2}$
20) $\frac{1}{4x^2y}$

21) $\frac{6}{7y^2}$
22) $\frac{3y^3}{2x^3}$
23) x^6y^6
24) $27x^9y^{12}$
25) $576x^4y^6$
26) $1,000x^3y^9$
27) $\frac{81}{x^4}$
28) $\frac{1}{36y^2}$
29) $\frac{y^3}{512x^6}$
30) $\frac{x^4}{4y^4}$
31) $\frac{x^4y^4}{16}$
32) $\frac{x^2y^2}{16}$
33) 16
34) 9
35) 343
36) $\frac{125}{8}$
37) $\frac{27}{8}$
38) $\frac{625}{81}$

39) $\frac{1}{x^7}$
40) $\frac{3}{y^5}$
41) $\frac{15}{y^3}$
42) $-\frac{20}{x^4}$
43) $\frac{12b^5}{a^3}$
44) $\frac{25a^3}{b^4c^3}$
45) $-\frac{4x^5}{y^3z^6}$
46) $\frac{18y^3}{x^3}$
47) $-\frac{5bc^4}{3a^2}$
48) 4.12×10^{-3}
49) 5.3×10^{-5}
50) 6.6×10^4
51) 7.2×10^7
52) 8
53) 3
54) 13
55) 10
56) 8
57) $9\sqrt{3}$

7 Expressions and Variables

Math topics that you'll learn in this chapter:

- ☑ Simplifying Variable Expressions
- ☑ Simplifying Polynomial Expressions
- ☑ The Distributive Property
- ☑ Evaluating One Variable
- ☑ Evaluating Two Variables

Simplifying Variable Expressions

- In algebra, a variable is a letter used to stand for a number. The most common letters are $x, y, z, a, b, c, m,$ and n.

- An algebraic expression is an expression that contains integers, variables, and math operations such as addition, subtraction, multiplication, division, etc.

- In an expression, we can combine "like" terms. (values with same variable and same power)

Examples:

Example 1. Simplify. $(4x + 2x + 4) =$

Solution: In this expression, there are three terms: $4x, 2x$, and 4. Two terms are "like terms": $4x$ and $2x$. Combine like terms. $4x + 2x = 6x$. Then: $(4x + 2x + 4) = 6x + 4$ (***remember you cannot combine variables and numbers.***)

Example 2. Simplify. $-2x^2 - 5x + 4x^2 - 9 =$

Solution: Combine "like" terms: $-2x^2 + 4x^2 = 2x^2$.
Then: $-2x^2 - 5x + 4x^2 - 9 = 2x^2 - 5x - 9$.

Example 3. Simplify. $(-8 + 6x^2 + 3x^2 + 9x) =$

Solution: Combine like terms. Then:
$(-8 + 6x^2 + 3x^2 + 9x) = 9x^2 + 9x - 8$

Example 4. Simplify. $-10x + 6x^2 - 3x + 9x^2 =$

Solution: Combine "like" terms: $-10x - 3x = -13x$, and $6x^2 + 9x^2 = 15x^2$
Then: $-10x + 6x^2 - 3x + 9x^2 = -13x + 15x^2$. Write in standard form (biggest powers first): $-13x + 15x^2 = 15x^2 - 13x$

Simplifying Polynomial Expressions

- In mathematics, a polynomial is an expression consisting of variables and coefficients that involves only the operations of addition, subtraction, multiplication, and non–negative integer exponents of variables. $P(x) = a_n x^n + a_{n-1} x^{n-1} + \dots + a_2 x^2 + a_1 x + a_0$

- Polynomials must always be simplified as much as possible. It means you must add together any like terms. (values with same variable and same power)

Examples:

Example 1. Simplify this Polynomial Expressions. $3x^2 - 6x^3 - 2x^3 + 4x^4$

Solution: Combine "like" terms: $-6x^3 - 2x^3 = -8x^3$
Then: $3x^2 - 6x^3 - 2x^3 + 4x^4 = 3x^2 - 8x^3 + 4x^4$
Now, write the expression in standard form: $4x^4 - 8x^3 + 3x^2$

Example 2. Simplify this expression. $(-5x^2 + 2x^3) - (3x^3 - 6x^2) =$

Solution: First, use distributive property: $\rightarrow$ multiply $(-)$ into $(3x^3 - 6x^2)$
$(-5x^2 + 2x^3) - (3x^3 - 6x^2) = -5x^2 + 2x^3 - 3x^3 + 6x^2$
Then combine "like" terms: $-5x^2 + 2x^3 - 3x^3 + 6x^2 = x^2 - x^3$
And write in standard form: $x^2 - x^3 = -x^3 + x^2$

Example 3. Simplify. $3x^3 - 9x^4 - 8x^2 + 12x^4 =$

Solution: Combine "like" terms:
$-9x^4 + 12x^4 = 3x^4$
Then: $3x^3 - 9x^4 - 8x^2 + 12x^4 = 3x^3 + 3x^4 - 8x^2$
And write in standard form: $3x^3 + 3x^4 - 8x^2 = 3x^4 + 3x^3 - 8x^2$

bit.ly/2WT5gtn

Find more at

The Distributive Property

- The distributive property (or the distributive property of multiplication over addition and subtraction) simplifies and solves expressions in the form of: $a(b + c)$ or $a(b - c)$

- The distributive property is multiplying a term outside the parentheses by the terms inside.

- Distributive Property rule: $a(b + c) = ab + ac$

Examples:

Example 1. Simply using the distributive property. $(-2)(x + 3)$

Solution: Use Distributive Property rule: $a(b + c) = ab + ac$
$(-2)(x + 3) = (-2 \times x) + (-2) \times (3) = -2x - 6$

Example 2. Simply. $(-5)(-2x - 6)$

Solution: Use Distributive Property rule: $a(b + c) = ab + ac$
$(-5)(-2x - 6) = (-5 \times -2x) + (-5) \times (-6) = 10x + 30$

Example 3. Simply. $(7)(2x - 8) - 12x$

Solution: First, simplify $(7)(2x - 8)$ using the distributive property.
Then: $(7)(2x - 8) = 14x - 56$
Now combine like terms: $(7)(2x - 8) - 12x = 14x - 56 - 12x$
In this expression, $14x$ and $-12x$ are "like terms" and we can combine them.
$14x - 12x = 2x$. Then: $14x - 56 - 12x = 2x - 56$

Evaluating One Variable

- To evaluate one variable expression, find the variable and substitute a number for that variable.

- Perform the arithmetic operations.

Examples:

Example 1. Calculate this expression for $x = 2$. $8 + 2x$

Solution: First, substitute 2 for x
Then: $8 + 2x = 8 + 2(2)$
Now, use order of operation to find the answer: $8 + 2(2) = 8 + 4 = 12$

Example 2. Evaluate this expression for $x = -1$. $4x - 8$

Solution: First, substitute -1 for x,
Then: $4x - 8 = 4(-1) - 8$
Now, use order of operation to find the answer: $4(-1) - 8 = -4 - 8 = -12$

Example 3. Find the value of this expression when $x = 4$. $16 - 5x$

Solution: First, substitute 4 for x,
Then: $16 - 5x = 16 - 5(4) = 16 - 20 = -4$

Example 4. Solve this expression for $x = -3$. $15 + 7x$

Solution: Substitute -3 for x,
Then: $15 + 7x = 15 + 7(-3) = 15 - 21 = -6$

Evaluating Two Variables

- To evaluate an algebraic expression, substitute a number for each variable.

- Perform the arithmetic operations to find the value of the expression.

Examples:

Example 1. Calculate this expression for a = 2 and $b = -1$. $4a - 3b$

Solution: First, substitute 2 for a, and -1 for b ,
*T*hen: $4a - 3b = 4(2) - 3(-1)$
Now, use order of operation to find the answer: $4(2) - 3(-1) = 8 + 3 = 11$

Example 2. Evaluate this expression for $x = -2$ and $y = 2$. $3x + 6y$

Solution: Substitute -2 for x, and 2 for y ,
Then: $3x + 6y = 3(-2) + 6(2) = -6 + 12 = 6$

Example 3. Find the value of this expression $2(6a - 5b)$ when $a = -1$ and $b = 4$.

Solution: Substitute -1 for a, and 4 for b ,
Then: $2(6a - 5b) = 12a - 10b = 12(-1) - 10(4) = -12 - 40 = -52$

Example 4. Solve this expression. $-7x - 2y$, $x = 4$, $y = -3$

Solution: Substitute 4 for x, and -3 for y and simplify.
Then: $-7x - 2y = -7(4) - 2(-3) = -28 + 6 = -22$

Chapter 7: Practices

✍ Simplify each expression.

1) $(3 + 4x - 1) =$

2) $(-5 - 2x + 7) =$

3) $(12x - 5x - 4) =$

4) $(-16x + 24x - 9) =$

5) $(6x + 5 - 15x) =$

6) $2 + 5x - 8x - 6 =$

7) $5x + 10 - 3x - 22 =$

8) $-5 - 3x^2 - 6 + 4x =$

9) $-6 + 9x^2 - 3 + x =$

10) $5x^2 + 3x - 10x - 3 =$

11) $4x^2 - 2x - 6x + 5 - 8 =$

12) $3x^2 - 5x - 7x + 2 - 4 =$

13) $9x^2 - x - 5x + 3 - 9 =$

14) $2x^2 - 7x - 3x^2 + 4x + 6 =$

✍ Simplify each polynomial.

15) $5x^2 + 3x^3 - 9x^2 + 2x =$ --

16) $8x^4 + 2x^5 - 7x^4 + 3x^2 =$ --

17) $15x^3 + 11x - 5x^2 - 9x^3 =$ --

18) $(7x^3 - 3x^2) + (5x^2 - 13x) =$ --

19) $(12x^4 + 6x^3) + (x^3 - 5x^4) =$ --

20) $(15x^5 - 8x^3) - (4x^3 + x^2) =$ --

21) $(14x^4 + 7x^3) - (x^3 - 24) =$ --

22) $(20x^4 + 6x^3) - (-x^3 - 2x^4) =$ --

23) $(x^2 + 9x^3) + (-22x^2 + 6x^3) =$ --

24) $(4x^4 - 2x^3) + (-5x^3 - 8x^4) =$ --

✍ Use the distributive property to simply each expression.

25) $2(6 + x) = $ _____

26) $5(3 - 2x) = $ _____

27) $7(1 - 5x) = $ _____

28) $(3 - 4x)7 = $ _____

29) $6(2 - 3x) = $ _____

30) $(-1)(-9 + x) = $ _____

31) $(-6)(3x - 2) = $ _____

32) $(-x + 12)(-4) = $ _____

33) $(-2)(1 - 6x) = $ _____

34) $(-5x - 3)(-8) = $ _____

✍ Evaluate each expression using the value given.

35) $x = 4 \rightarrow 10 - x = $ ____

36) $x = 6 \rightarrow x + 8 = $ ____

37) $x = 3 \rightarrow 2x - 6 = $ ____

38) $x = 2 \rightarrow 10 - 4x = $ ____

39) $x = 7 \rightarrow 8x - 3 = $ ____

40) $x = 9 \rightarrow 20 - 2x = $ ____

41) $x = 5 \rightarrow 10x - 30 = $ ___

42) $x = -6 \rightarrow 5 - x = $ ____

43) $x = -3 \rightarrow 22 - 3x = $ ____

44) $x = -7 \rightarrow 10 - 9x = $ ____

45) $x = -10 \rightarrow 40 - 3x = $ ____

46) $x = -2 \rightarrow 20x - 5 = $ ____

47) $x = -5 \rightarrow -10x - 8 = $ ___

48) $x = -4 \rightarrow -1 - 4x = $ ___

✍ Evaluate each expression using the values given.

49) $x = 2, y = 1 \rightarrow 2x + 7y = $ _____

50) $a = 3, b = 5 \rightarrow 3a - 5b = $ _____

51) $x = 6, y = 2 \rightarrow 3x - 2y + 8 = $ _____

52) $a = -2, b = 3 \rightarrow -5a + 2b + 6 = $ _____

53) $x = -4, y = -3 \rightarrow -4x + 10 - 8y = $ _____

Chapter 7: Answers

1) $4x + 2$

2) $-2x + 2$

3) $7x - 4$

4) $8x - 9$

5) $-9x + 5$

6) $-3x - 4$

7) $2x - 12$

8) $-3x^2 + 4x - 11$

9) $9x^2 + x - 9$

10) $5x^2 - 7x - 3$

11) $4x^2 - 8x - 3$

12) $3x^2 - 12x - 2$

13) $9x^2 - 6x - 6$

14) $-x^2 - 3x + 6$

15) $3x^3 - 4x^2 + 2x$

16) $2x^5 + x^4 + 3x^2$

17) $6x^3 - 5x^2 + 11x$

18) $7x^3 + 2x^2 - 13x$

19) $7x^4 + 7x^3$

20) $15x^5 - 12x^3 - x^2$

21) $14x^4 + 6x^3 + 24$

22) $22x^4 + 7x^3$

23) $15x^3 - 21x^2$

24) $-4x^4 - 7x^3$

25) $2x + 12$

26) $-10x + 15$

27) $-35x + 7$

28) $-28x + 21$

29) $-18x + 12$

30) $-x + 9$

31) $-18x + 12$

32) $4x - 48$

33) $12x - 2$

34) $40x + 24$

35) 6

36) 14

37) 0

38) 2

39) 53

40) 2

41) 20

42) 11

43) 31

44) 73

45) 70

46) -45

47) 42

48) 15

49) 11

50) -16

51) 22

52) 22

53) 50

CHAPTER

8 Equations and Inequalities

Math topics that you'll learn in this chapter:

- ☑ One-Step Equations
- ☑ Multi-Step Equations
- ☑ System of Equations
- ☑ Graphing Single–Variable Inequalities
- ☑ One-Step Inequalities
- ☑ Multi-Step Inequalities

One–Step Equations

- The values of two expressions on both sides of an equation are equal. Example: $ax = b$. In this equation, ax is equal to b.

- Solving an equation means finding the value of the variable.

- You only need to perform one Math operation to solve the one-step equations.

- To solve a one-step equation, find the inverse (opposite) operation is being performed.

- The inverse operations are:

  ❖ Addition and subtraction

  ❖ Multiplication and division

Examples:

Example 1. Solve this equation for x. $4x = 16, x = ?$

Solution: Here, the operation is multiplication (variable x is multiplied by 4) and its inverse operation is division. To solve this equation, divide both sides of equation by 4: $4x = 16 \rightarrow \frac{4x}{4} = \frac{16}{4} \rightarrow x = 4$

Example 2. Solve this equation. $x + 8 = 0$, $x = ?$

Solution: In this equation 8 is added to the variable x. The inverse operation of addition is subtraction. To solve this equation, subtract 8 from both sides of the equation: $x + 8 - 8 = 0 - 8$. Then: $\rightarrow x = -8$

Example 3. Solve this equation for x. $x - 12 = 0$

Solution: Here, the operation is subtraction and its inverse operation is addition. To solve this equation, add 12 to both sides of the equation:
$x - 12 + 12 = 0 + 12 \rightarrow x = 12$

Multi–Step Equations

- To solve a multi-step equation, combine "like" terms on one side.

- Bring variables to one side by adding or subtracting.

- Simplify using the inverse of addition or subtraction.

- Simplify further by using the inverse of multiplication or division.

- Check your solution by plugging the value of the variable into the original equation.

Examples:

Example 1. Solve this equation for x. $4x + 8 = 20 - 2x$

Solution: First, bring variables to one side by adding $2x$ to both sides. Then: $4x + 8 + 2x = 20 - 2x + 2x \rightarrow 4x + 8 + 2x = 20$.

Simplify: $6x + 8 = 20$ Now, subtract 8 from both sides of the equation:

$6x + 8 - 8 = 20 - 8 \rightarrow 6x = 12 \rightarrow$ Divide both sides by 6:

$6x = 12 \rightarrow \dfrac{6x}{6} = \dfrac{12}{6} \rightarrow x = 2$

Let's check this solution by substituting the value of 2 for x in the original equation:

$x = 2 \rightarrow 4x + 8 = 20 - 2x \rightarrow 4(2) + 8 = 20 - 2(2) \rightarrow 16 = 16$

The answer $x = 2$ is correct.

Example 2. Solve this equation for x. $-5x + 4 = 24$

Solution: Subtract 4 from both sides of the equation.

$-5x + 4 = 24 \rightarrow -5x + 4 - 4 = 24 - 4 \rightarrow -5x = 20$

Divide both sides by -5, then: $-5x = 20 \rightarrow \dfrac{-5x}{-5} = \dfrac{20}{-5} \rightarrow x = -4$

Now, check the solution:

$x = -4 \rightarrow -5x + 4 = 24 \rightarrow -5(-4) + 4 = 24 \rightarrow 24 = 24$

The answer $x = -4$ is correct.

System of Equations

- A system of equations contains two equations and two variables. For example, consider the system of equations: $x - y = 1, x + y = 5$

- The easiest way to solve a system of equations is using the elimination method. The elimination method uses the addition property of equality. You can add the same value to each side of an equation.

- For the first equation above, you can add $x + y$ to the left side and 5 to the right side of the first equation: $x - y + (x + y) = 1 + 5$. Now, if you simplify, you get: $x - y + (x + y) = 1 + 5 \rightarrow 2x = 6 \rightarrow x = 3$. Now, substitute 3 for the x in the first equation: $3 - y = 1$. By solving this equation, $y = 2$

Example:

Example 1. What is the value of $x + y$ in this system of equations?

$$\begin{cases} 2x + 4y = 12 \\ 4x - 2y = -16 \end{cases}$$

Solution: Solving a System of Equations by Elimination:
Multiply the first equation by (-2), then add it to the second equation.

$$\begin{matrix} -2(2x + 4y = 12) \\ 4x - 2y = -16 \end{matrix} \Rightarrow \begin{matrix} -4x - 8y = -24 \\ 4x - 2y = -16 \end{matrix} \Rightarrow -10y = -40 \Rightarrow y = 4$$

Plug in the value of y into one of the equations and solve for x.
$2x + 4(4) = 12 \Rightarrow 2x + 16 = 12 \Rightarrow 2x = -4 \Rightarrow x = -2$
Thus, $x + y = -2 + 4 = 2$

bit.ly/3mPGO6k

Find more at

Graphing Single–Variable Inequalities

-   An inequality compares two expressions using an inequality sign.

-   Inequality signs are: "less than" <, "greater than" >, "less than or equal to" ≤, and "greater than or equal to" ≥.

-   To graph a single–variable inequality, find the value of the inequality on the number line.

-   For less than (<) or greater than (>) draw an open circle on the value of the variable. If there is an equal sign too, then use a filled circle.

-   Draw an arrow to the right for greater or to the left for less than.

Examples:

Example 1. Draw a graph for this inequality. $x > 2$

Solution: Since the variable is greater than 2, then we need to find 2 in the number line and draw an open circle on it. Then, draw an arrow to the right.

Example 2. Graph this inequality. $x \leq -3$.

Solution: Since the variable is less than or equal to −3, then we need to find −3 in the number line and draw a filled circle on it. Then, draw an arrow to the left.

bit.ly/3aJ4GGo

Find more at

One–Step Inequalities

- An inequality compares two expressions using an inequality sign.

- Inequality signs are: "less than" <, "greater than" >, "less than or equal to" ≤, and "greater than or equal to" ≥.

- You only need to perform one Math operation to solve the one-step inequalities.

- To solve one-step inequalities, find the inverse (opposite) operation is being performed.

- For dividing or multiplying both sides by negative numbers, flip the direction of the inequality sign.

Examples:

Example 1. Solve this inequality for x. $x + 5 \geq 4$

Solution: The inverse (opposite) operation of addition is subtraction. In this inequality, 5 is added to x. To isolate x we need to subtract 5 from both sides of the inequality.
Then: $x + 5 \geq 4 \rightarrow x + 5 - 5 \geq 4 - 5 \rightarrow x \geq -1$. The solution is: $x \geq -1$

Example 2. Solve the inequality. $x - 3 > -6$.

Solution: 3 is subtracted from x. Add 3 to both sides.
$x - 3 > -6 \rightarrow x - 3 + 3 > -6 + 3 \rightarrow x > -3$

Example 3. Solve. $4x \leq -8$.

Solution: 4 is multiplied to x. Divide both sides by 4.
Then: $4x \leq -8 \rightarrow \frac{4x}{4} \leq \frac{-8}{4} \rightarrow x \leq -2$

Example 4. Solve. $-3x \leq 6$.

Solution: -3 is multiplied to x. Divide both sides by -3. Remember when dividing or multiplying both sides of an inequality by negative numbers, flip the direction of the inequality sign.
Then: $-3x \leq 6 \rightarrow \frac{-3x}{-3} \geq \frac{6}{-3} \rightarrow x \geq -2$

bit.ly/3rrEIgL

Find more at

Multi–Step Inequalities

- To solve a multi-step inequality, combine "like" terms on one side.

- Bring variables to one side by adding or subtracting.

- Isolate the variable.

- Simplify using the inverse of addition or subtraction.

- Simplify further by using the inverse of multiplication or division.

- For dividing or multiplying both sides by negative numbers, flip the direction of the inequality sign.

Examples:

Example 1. Solve this inequality. $8x - 2 \leq 14$

Solution: In this inequality, 2 is subtracted from $8x$. The inverse of subtraction is addition. Add 2 to both sides of the inequality:

$8x - 2 + 2 \leq 14 + 2 \rightarrow 8x \leq 16$

Now, divide both sides by 8. Then: $8x \leq 16 \rightarrow \frac{8x}{8} \leq \frac{16}{8} \rightarrow x \leq 2$

The solution of this inequality is $x \leq 2$.

Example 2. Solve this inequality. $3x + 9 < 12$

Solution: First, subtract 9 from both sides: $3x + 9 - 9 < 12 - 9$

Then simplify: $3x + 9 - 9 < 12 - 9 \rightarrow 3x < 3$

Now divide both sides by 3: $\frac{3x}{3} < \frac{3}{3} \rightarrow x < 1$

Example 3. Solve this inequality. $-5x + 3 \geq 8$

Solution: First, subtract 3 from both sides:

$-5x + 3 - 3 \geq 8 - 3 \rightarrow -5x \geq 5$

Divide both sides by -5. Remember that you need to flip the direction of inequality sign. $-5x \geq 5 \rightarrow \frac{-5x}{-5} \leq \frac{5}{-5} \rightarrow x \leq -1$

Chapter 8: Practices

✍ Solve each equation. (One−Step Equations)

1) $x + 6 = 3 \rightarrow x = \underline{\hspace{1cm}}$ ...

2) $5 = 11 - x \rightarrow x = \underline{\hspace{1cm}}$

3) $-3 = 8 + x \rightarrow x = \underline{\hspace{1cm}}$

4) $x - 2 = -7 \rightarrow x = \underline{\hspace{1cm}}$

5) $-15 = x + 6 \rightarrow x = \underline{\hspace{1cm}}$

6) $10 - x = -2 \rightarrow x = \underline{\hspace{1cm}}$

7) $22 - x = -9 \rightarrow x = \underline{\hspace{1cm}}$

8) $-4 + x = 28 \rightarrow x = \underline{\hspace{1cm}}$

9) $11 - x = -7 \rightarrow x = \underline{\hspace{1cm}}$

10) $35 - x = -7 \rightarrow x = \underline{\hspace{1cm}}$

✍ Solve each equation. (Multi−Step Equations)

11) $4(x + 2) = 12 \rightarrow x = \underline{\hspace{1cm}}$

12) $-6(6 - x) = 12 \rightarrow x = \underline{\hspace{1cm}}$

13) $5 = -5(x + 2) \rightarrow x = \underline{\hspace{1cm}}$

14) $-10 = 2(4 + x) \rightarrow x = \underline{\hspace{1cm}}$

15) $4(x + 2) = -12, x = \underline{\hspace{1cm}}$

16) $-6(3 + 2x) = 30, x = \underline{\hspace{1cm}}$

17) $-3(4 - x) = 12, x = \underline{\hspace{1cm}}$

18) $-4(6 - x) = 16, x = \underline{\hspace{1cm}}$

✍ Solve each system of equations.

19) $\begin{cases} x + 6y = 32 \\ x + 3y = 17 \end{cases}$ $x = \underline{\hspace{1cm}}$ $y = \underline{\hspace{1cm}}$

20) $\begin{cases} 3x + y = 15 \\ x + 2y = 10 \end{cases}$ $x = \underline{\hspace{1cm}}$ $y = \underline{\hspace{1cm}}$

21) $\begin{cases} 3x + 5y = 17 \\ 2x + y = 9 \end{cases}$ $x = \underline{\hspace{1cm}}$ $y = \underline{\hspace{1cm}}$

22) $\begin{cases} 5x - 2y = -8 \\ -6x + 2y = 10 \end{cases}$ $x = \underline{\hspace{1cm}}$ $y = \underline{\hspace{1cm}}$

✍ Draw a graph for each inequality.

23) $x \le -3$

24) $x > -5$

✍ Solve each inequality and graph it.

25) $x - 2 \ge -2$

26) $2x - 3 < 9$

✍ Solve each inequality.

27) $x + 13 > 4$

28) $x + 6 > 5$

29) $-12 + 2x \le 26$

30) $-2 + 8x \le 14$

31) $6 + 4x \le 18$

32) $4(x + 3) \ge -12$

33) $2(6 + x) \ge -12$

34) $3(x - 5) < -6$

35) $10 + 5x < -15$

36) $6(6 + x) \ge -18$

37) $2(x - 5) \ge -14$

38) $6(x + 4) < -12$

39) $3(x - 8) \ge -48$

40) $-(6 - 4x) > -30$

41) $2(2 + 2x) > -60$

42) $-3(4 + 2x) > -24$

Chapter 8: Answers

1) -3

2) 6

3) -11

4) -5

5) -21

6) 12

7) 31

8) 32

9) 18

10) 42

11) 1

12) 8

13) -3

14) -9

15) -5

16) -4

17) 8

18) 10

19) $x = 2, y = 5$

20) $x = 4, y = 3$

21) $x = 4, y = 1$

22) $x = -2, y = -1$

23) $x \leq -3$

24) $x > -5$

25) $x \geq 0$

26) $x < 6$

27) $x > -9$

28) $x > -1$

29) $x \leq 19$

30) $x \leq 2$

31) $x \leq 3$

32) $x \geq -6$

33) $x \geq -12$

34) $x < 3$

35) $x < -5$

36) $x \geq -9$

37) $x \geq -2$

38) $x < -6$

39) $x \geq -8$

40) $x > -6$

41) $x > -16$

42) $x < 2$

CHAPTER

9 Lines and Slope

Math topics that you'll learn in this chapter:

- ☑ Finding Slope
- ☑ Graphing Lines Using Slope–Intercept Form
- ☑ Writing Linear Equations
- ☑ Finding Midpoint
- ☑ Finding Distance of Two Points
- ☑ Graphing Linear Inequalities

Finding Slope

- The slope of a line represents the direction of a line on the coordinate plane.

- A coordinate plane contains two perpendicular number lines. The horizontal line is x and the vertical line is y. The point at which the two axes intersect is called the origin. An ordered pair (x, y) shows the location of a point.

- A line on a coordinate plane can be drawn by connecting two points.

- To find the slope of a line, we need the equation of the line or two points on the line.

- The slope of a line with two points A (x_1, y_1) and B (x_2, y_2) can be found by using this formula: $\frac{y_2 - y_1}{x_2 - x_1} = \frac{rise}{run}$

- The equation of a line is typically written as $y = mx + b$ where m is the slope and b is the y-intercept.

Examples:

Example 1. Find the slope of the line through these two points:

A$(1, -6)$ and $B(3, 2)$.

Solution: Slope $= \frac{y_2 - y_1}{x_2 - x_1}$. Let (x_1, y_1) be A$(1, -6)$ and (x_2, y_2) be $B(3, 2)$.
(Remember, you can choose any point for (x_1, y_1) and (x_2, y_2)).
Then: slope $= \frac{y_2 - y_1}{x_2 - x_1} = \frac{2 - (-6)}{3 - 1} = \frac{8}{2} = 4$

The slope of the line through these two points is 4.

Example 2. Find the slope of the line with equation $y = -2x + 8$

Solution: when the equation of a line is written in the form of $y = mx + b$, the slope is m. In this line: $y = -2x + 8$, the slope is -2.

Graphing Lines Using Slope–Intercept Form

- Slope–intercept form of a line: given the slope m and the y-intercept (the intersection of the line and y-axis) b, then the equation of the line is:

$$y = mx + b$$

- To draw the graph of a linear equation in a slope-intercept form on the xy coordinate plane, find two points on the line by plugging two values for x and calculating the values of y.

- You can also use the slope (m) and one point to graph the line.

Example:

Example 1. Sketch the graph of $y = 2x - 4$.

Solution: To graph this line, we need to find two points. When x is zero the value of y is -4. And when x is 2 the value of y is 0.

$$x = 0 \rightarrow y = 2(0) - 4 = -4,$$
$$y = 0 \rightarrow 0 = 2x - 4 \rightarrow x = 2$$

Now, we have two points:
$(0, -4)$ and $(2, 0)$.
Find the points on the coordinate plane and graph the line. Remember that the slope of the line is 2.

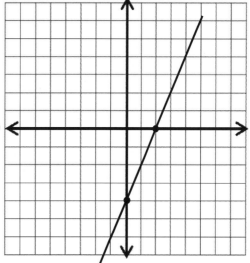

Writing Linear Equations

- The equation of a line in slope-intercept form: $y = mx + b$

- To write the equation of a line, first identify the slope.

- Find the y-intercept. This can be done by substituting the slope and the coordinates of a point (x, y) on the line.

Examples:

Example 1. What is the equation of the line that passes through $(3, -4)$ and has a slope of 6?

Solution: The general slope-intercept form of the equation of a line is
$y = mx + b$, where m is the slope and b is the y-intercept.
By substitution of the given point and given slope:
$y = mx + b \rightarrow -4 = (3)(6) + b$. So, $b = -4 - 18 = -22$, and the required equation
is $y = 6x - 22$

Example 2. Write the equation of the line through two points $A(3,1)$ and $B(-2, 6)$.

Solution: First, find the slope: $Slop = \frac{y_2 - y_1}{x_2 - x_1} = \frac{6 - 1}{-2 - 3} = \frac{5}{-5} = -1 \rightarrow m = -1$
To find the value of b, use either points and plug in the values of x and y in the equation. The answer will be the same: $y = -x + b$. Let's check both points.
Then: $(3,1) \rightarrow y = mx + b \rightarrow 1 = -1(3) + b \rightarrow b = 4$
$(-2,6) \rightarrow y = mx + b \rightarrow 6 = -1(-2) + b \rightarrow b = 4$.
The y-intercept of the line is 4. The equation of the line is: $y = -x + 4$

Example 3. What is the equation of the line that passes through $(4, -1)$ and has a slope of 4?

Solution: The general slope-intercept form of the equation of a line is
$y = mx + b$, where m is the slope and b is the y-intercept. By substitution of the given point and given slope: $y = mx + b \rightarrow -1 = (4)(4) + b$
So, $b = -1 - 16 = -17$, and the equation of the line is: $y = 4x - 17$.

Finding Midpoint

- The middle of a line segment is its midpoint.

- The Midpoint of two endpoints A (x_1, y_1) and B (x_2, y_2) can be found using this formula: M $(\frac{x_1+x_2}{2}, \frac{y_1+y_2}{2})$

Examples:

Example 1. Find the midpoint of the line segment with the given endpoints. $(2, -4), (6, 8)$

Solution: Midpoint $= \left(\frac{x_1+x_2}{2}, \frac{y_1+y_2}{2}\right) \rightarrow (x_1, y_1) = (2, -4)$ and $(x_2, y_2) = (6, 8)$

Midpoint $= \left(\frac{2+6}{2}, \frac{-4+8}{2}\right) \rightarrow \left(\frac{8}{2}, \frac{4}{2}\right) \rightarrow M(4, 2)$

Example 2. Find the midpoint of the line segment with the given endpoints. $(-2, 3), (6, -7)$

Solution: Midpoint $= \left(\frac{x_1+x_2}{2}, \frac{y_1+y_2}{2}\right) \rightarrow (x_1, y_1) = (-2, 3)$ and $(x_2, y_2) = (6, -7)$

Midpoint $= \left(\frac{-2+6}{2}, \frac{3-7}{2}\right) \rightarrow \left(\frac{4}{2}, \frac{-4}{2}\right) \rightarrow M(2, -2)$

Example 3. Find the midpoint of the line segment with the given endpoints. $(7, -4), (1, 8)$

Solution: Midpoint $= \left(\frac{x_1+x_2}{2}, \frac{y_1+y_2}{2}\right) \rightarrow (x_1, y_1) = (7, -4)$ and $(x_2, y_2) = (1, 8)$

Midpoint $= \left(\frac{7+1}{2}, \frac{-4+8}{2}\right) \rightarrow \left(\frac{8}{2}, \frac{4}{2}\right) \rightarrow M(4, 2)$

Example 4. Find the midpoint of the line segment with the given endpoints. $(6, 3), (10, -9)$

Solution: Midpoint $= \left(\frac{x_1+x_2}{2}, \frac{y_1+y_2}{2}\right) \rightarrow (x_1, y_1) = (6, 3)$ and $(x_2, y_2) = (10, -9)$

Midpoint $= \left(\frac{6+10}{2}, \frac{3-9}{2}\right) \rightarrow \left(\frac{16}{2}, \frac{-6}{2}\right) \rightarrow M(8, -3)$

bit.ly/3nPdnTq
Find more at

Finding Distance of Two Points

- Use the following formula to find the distance of two points with the coordinates A (x_1, y_1) and B (x_2, y_2):

$$d = \sqrt{(x_2 - x_1)^2 + (y_2 - y_1)^2}$$

Examples:

Example 1. Find the distance between $(4, 2)$ and $(-5, -10)$.

Solution: Use distance of two points formula: $d = \sqrt{(x_2 - x_1)^2 + (y_2 - y_1)^2}$
$(x_1, y_1) = (4, 2)$ and $(x_2, y_2) = (-5, -10)$. Then: $d = \sqrt{(x_2 - x_1)^2 + (y_2 - y_1)^2} \rightarrow$
$= \sqrt{(-5 - 4)^2 + (-10 - 2)^2} = \sqrt{(-9)^2 + (-12)^2} = \sqrt{81 + 144} = \sqrt{225} = 15$
Then: $d = 15$

Example 2. Find the distance of two points $(-1, 5)$ and $(-3, -6)$.

Solution: Use distance of two points formula: $d = \sqrt{(x_2 - x_1)^2 + (y_2 - y_1)^2}$
$(x_1, y_1) = (-1, 5)$, and $(x_2, y_2) = (-3, -6)$
Then: $= \sqrt{(x_2 - x_1)^2 + (y_2 - y_1)^2} \rightarrow d = \sqrt{(-3 - (-1))^2 + (-6 - (5))^2} =$
$\sqrt{(-2)^2 + (-11)^2} = \sqrt{4 + 121} = \sqrt{125} = 5\sqrt{5}$. Then: $d = 5\sqrt{5}$

Example 3. Find the distance between $(-6, 5)$ and $(-2, 2)$.

Solution: Use distance of two points formula: $d = \sqrt{(x_2 - x_1)^2 + (y_2 - y_1)^2}$
$(x_1, y_1) = (-6, 5)$ and $(x_2, y_2) = (-2, 2)$. Then: $d = \sqrt{(x_2 - x_1)^2 + (y_2 - y_1)^2}$
$d = \sqrt{(-2 - (-6))^2 + (2 - 5)^2} = \sqrt{(4)^2 + (-3)^2} = \sqrt{16 + 9} = \sqrt{25} = 5$

Graphing Linear Inequalities

- To graph a linear inequality, first draw a graph of the "equals" line.

- Use a dash line for less than (<) and greater than (>) signs and a solid line for less than and equal to (≤) and greater than and equal to (≥).

- Choose a testing point. (it can be any point on both sides of the line.)

- Put the value of (x, y) of that point in the inequality. If that works, that part of the line is the solution. If the values don't work, then the other part of the line is the solution.

Example:

Sketch the graph of inequality: $y < 2x + 4$

Solution: To draw the graph of $y < 2x + 4$, you first need to graph the line:

$y = 2x + 4$

Since there is a less than (<) sign, draw a dash line.

The slope is 2 and y-intercept is 4.

Then, choose a testing point and substitute the value of x and y from that point into the inequality. The easiest point to test is the origin: $(0, 0)$

$(0,0) \rightarrow y < 2x + 4 \rightarrow 0 < 2(0) + 4 \rightarrow 0 < 4$

This is correct! 0 is less than 4. So, this part of the line (on the right side) is the solution of this inequality.

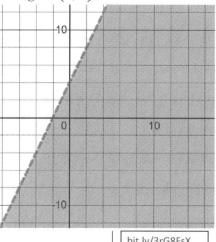

bit.ly/3rG8FsX

Find more at

Chapter 9: Practices

✍ Find the slope of each line.

1) $y = x - 5$

2) $y = 2x + 6$

3) $y = -5x - 8$

4) Line through $(2, 6)$ *and* $(5, 0)$

5) Line through $(8, 0)$ *and* $(-4, 3)$

6) Line through $(-2, -4)$ *and* $(-4, 8)$

✍ Sketch the graph of each line. (Using Slope−Intercept Form)

7) $y = x + 4$

8) $y = 2x - 5$

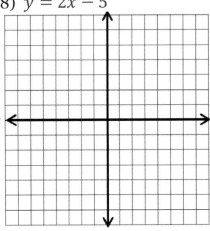

✍ Solve.

9) What is the equation of a line with slope 4 and intercept 16? _____

10) What is the equation of a line with slope 3 and passes through point $(1, 5)$?

_____

11) What is the equation of a line with slope -5 and passes through point $(-2, 7)$?

_____

12) The slope of a line is -4 and it passes through point $(-6, 2)$. What is the equation of the line? _____

13) The slope of a line is -3 and it passes through point $(-3, -6)$. What is the equation of the line? _____

 Sketch the graph of each linear inequality.

14) $y > 2x - 2$

15) $y < -x + 3$

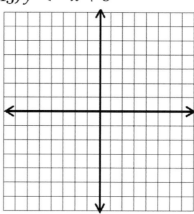

Find the midpoint of the line segment with the given endpoints.

16) $(5, 0), (1, 4)$

17) $(2, 3), (4, 7)$

18) $(8, 1), (2, 5)$

19) $(5, 10), (3, 6)$

20) $(4, -1), (-2, 7)$

21) $(2, -5), (4, 1)$

22) $(7, 6), (-5, 2)$

23) $(-2, 8), (4, -6)$

Find the distance between each pair of points.

24) $(-2, 8), (-6, 8)$

25) $(4, -4), (14, 20)$

26) $(-1, 9), (-5, 6)$

27) $(0, 3), (4, 3)$

28) $(0, -2), (5, 10)$

29) $(4, 3), (7, -1)$

30) $(2, 6), (10, -9)$

31) $(3, 3), (6, -1)$

32) $(-2, -12), (14, 18)$

33) $(2, -2), (12, 22)$

Chapter 9: Answers

1) 1

2) 2

3) −5

4) −2

5) $-\frac{1}{4}$

6) −6

7) $y = x + 4$

8) $y = 2x − 5$

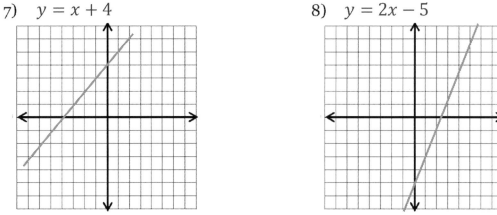

9) $y = 4x + 16$

10) $y = 3x + 2$

11) $y = −5x − 3$

12) $y = −4x − 22$

13) $y = −3x − 15$

14) $y > 2x − 2$

15) $y < −x + 3$

16) $(3,2)$

17) $(3,5)$

18) $(5,3)$

19) $(4,8)$

20) $(1,3)$

21) $(3,−2)$

22) $(1,4)$

23) $(1,1)$

24) 4

25) 26

26) 5

27) 4

28) 13

29) 5

30) 17

31) 5

32) 34

33) 26

CHAPTER

10 Polynomials

Math topics that you'll learn in this chapter:

- ☑ Simplifying Polynomials
- ☑ Adding and Subtracting Polynomials
- ☑ Multiplying Monomials
- ☑ Multiplying and Dividing Monomials
- ☑ Multiplying a Polynomial and a Monomial
- ☑ Multiplying Binomials
- ☑ Factoring Trinomials

Simplifying Polynomials

- To simplify Polynomials, find "like" terms. (they have same variables with same power).

- Use "FOIL". (First–Out–In–Last) for binomials:

$$(x + a)(x + b) = x^2 + (b + a)x + ab$$

- Add or Subtract "like" terms using order of operation.

Examples:

Example 1. Simplify this expression. $x(4x + 7) - 2x =$

Solution: Use Distributive Property: $x(4x + 7) = 4x^2 + 7x$
Now, combine like terms: $x(4x + 7) - 2x = 4x^2 + 7x - 2x = 4x^2 + 5x$

Example 2. Simplify this expression. $(x + 3)(x + 5) =$

Solution: First, apply the FOIL method: $(a + b)(c + d) = ac + ad + bc + bd$
$(x + 3)(x + 5) = x^2 + 5x + 3x + 15$
Now combine like terms: $x^2 + 5x + 3x + 15 = x^2 + 8x + 15$

Example 3. Simplify this expression. $2x(x - 5) - 3x^2 + 6x =$

Solution: Use Distributive Property: $2x(x - 5) = 2x^2 - 10x$
Then: $2x(x - 5) - 3x^2 + 6x = 2x^2 - 10x - 3x^2 + 6x$
Now combine like terms: $2x^2 - 3x^2 = -x^2$, and $-10x + 6x = -4x$
The simplified form of the expression: $2x^2 - 10x - 3x^2 + 6 = -x^2 - 4x$

Adding and Subtracting Polynomials

- Adding polynomials is just a matter of combining like terms, with some order of operations considerations thrown in.

- Be careful with the minus signs, and don't confuse addition and multiplication!

- For subtracting polynomials, sometimes you need to use the Distributive Property: $a(b + c) = ab + ac$, $a(b - c) = ab - ac$

Examples:

Example 1. Simplify the expressions. $(x^2 - 2x^3) - (x^3 - 3x^2) =$

Solution: First, use Distributive Property:
$$-(x^3 - 3x^2) = -x^3 + 3x^2$$
$\rightarrow (x^2 - 2x^3) - (x^3 - 3x^2) = x^2 - 2x^3 - x^3 + 3x^2$
Now combine like terms: $-2x^3 - x^3 = -3x^3$ and $x^2 + 3x^2 = 4x^2$
Then: $(x^2 - 2x^3) - (x^3 - 3x^2) = x^2 - 2x^3 - x^3 + 3x^2 = -3x^3 + 4x^2$

Example 2. Add expressions. $(3x^3 - 5) + (4x^3 - 2x^2) =$

Solution: Remove parentheses:
$(3x^3 - 5) + (4x^3 - 2x^2) = 3x^3 - 5 + 4x^3 - 2x^2$
Now combine like terms: $3x^3 - 5 + 4x^3 - 2x^2 = 7x^3 - 2x^2 - 5$

Example 3. Simplify the expressions. $(-4x^2 - 2x^3) - (5x^2 + 2x^3) =$

Solution: First, use Distributive Property:
$-(5x^2 + 2x^3) = -5x^2 - 2x^3 \rightarrow (-4x^2 - 2x^3) - (5x^2 + 2x^3)$
$$= -4x^2 - 2x^3 - 5x^2 - 2x^3$$
Now combine like terms and write in standard form:
$-4x^2 - 2x^3 - 5x^2 - 2x^3 = -4x^3 - 9x^2$

Multiplying Monomials

- A monomial is a polynomial with just one term: Examples: $2x$ or $7y^2$.

- When you multiply monomials, first multiply the coefficients (a number placed before and multiplying the variable) and then multiply the variables using multiplication property of exponents.

$$x^a \times x^b = x^{a+b}$$

Examples:

Example 1. Multiply expressions. $2xy^3 \times 6x^4y^2$

Solution: Find the same variables and use multiplication property of exponents: $x^a \times x^b = x^{a+b}$

$x \times x^4 = x^{1+4} = x^5$ and $y^3 \times y^2 = y^{3+2} = y^5$

Then, multiply coefficients and variables: $2xy^3 \times 6x^4y^2 = 12x^5y^5$

Example 2. Multiply expressions. $7a^3b^8 \times 3a^6b^4 =$

Solution: Use the multiplication property of exponents: $x^a \times x^b = x^{a+b}$

$a^3 \times a^6 = a^{3+6} = a^9$ and $b^8 \times b^4 = b^{8+4} = b^{12}$

Then: $7a^3b^8 \times 3a^6b^4 = 21a^9b^{12}$

Example 3. Multiply. $5x^2y^4z^3 \times 4x^4y^7z^5$

Solution: Use the multiplication property of exponents: $x^a \times x^b = x^{a+b}$

$x^2 \times x^4 = x^{2+4} = x^6$, $y^4 \times y^7 = y^{4+7} = y^{11}$ and $z^3 \times z^5 = z^{3+5} = z^8$

Then: $5x^2y^4z^3 \times 4x^4y^7z^5 = 20x^6y^{11}z^8$

Example 4. Simplify. $(-6a^7b^4)(4a^8b^5) =$

Solution: Use the multiplication property of exponents: $x^a \times x^b = x^{a+b}$

$a^7 \times a^8 = a^{7+8} = a^{15}$ and $b^4 \times b^5 = b^{4+5} = b^9$

Then: $(-6a^7b^4)(4a^8b^5) = -24a^{15}b^9$

bit.ly/2KLVoP8

Find more at

Multiplying and Dividing Monomials

- When you divide or multiply two monomials, you need to divide or multiply their coefficients and then divide or multiply their variables.

- In case of exponents with the same base, for Division, subtract their powers, for Multiplication, add their powers.

- Exponent's Multiplication and Division rules:

$$x^a \times x^b = x^{a+b}, \qquad \frac{x^a}{x^b} = x^{a-b}$$

Examples:

Example 1. Multiply expressions. $(3x^5)(9x^4) =$

Solution: Use multiplication property of exponents:
$x^a \times x^b = x^{a+b} \rightarrow x^5 \times x^4 = x^9$
Then: $(3x^5)(9x^4) = 27x^9$

Example 2. Divide expressions. $\frac{12x^4y^6}{6xy^2} =$

Solution: Use division property of exponents:
$\frac{x^a}{x^b} = x^{a-b} \rightarrow \frac{x^4}{x} = x^{4-1} = x^3$ and $\frac{y^6}{y^2} = y^{6-2} = y^4$
Then: $\frac{12x^4y^6}{6xy^2} = 2x^3y^4$

Example 3. Divide expressions. $\frac{49a^6b^9}{7a^3b^4} =$

Solution: Use division property of exponents:
$\frac{x^a}{x^b} = x^{a-b} \rightarrow \frac{a^6}{a^3} = a^{6-3} = a^3$ and $\frac{b^9}{b^4} = b^{9-4} = b^5$
Then: $\frac{49a^6b^9}{7a^3b^4} = 7a^3b^5$

bit.ly/2WHp4Q4

Find more at

Multiplying a Polynomial and a Monomial

- When multiplying monomials, use the product rule for exponents.

$$x^a \times x^b = x^{a+b}$$

- When multiplying a monomial by a polynomial, use the distributive property.

$$a \times (b + c) = a \times b + a \times c = ab + ac$$
$$a \times (b - c) = a \times b - a \times c = ab - ac$$

Examples:

Example 1. Multiply expressions. $6x(2x + 5)$

Solution: Use Distributive Property:

$6x(2x + 5) = 6x \times 2x + 6x \times 5 = 12x^2 + 30x$

Example 2. Multiply expressions. $x(3x^2 + 4y^2)$

Solution: Use Distributive Property:

$x(3x^2 + 4y^2) = x \times 3x^2 + x \times 4y^2 = 3x^3 + 4xy^2$

Example 3. Multiply. $-x(-2x^2 + 4x + 5)$

Solution: Use Distributive Property:

$-x(-2x^2 + 4x + 5) = (-x)(-2x^2) + (-x) \times (4x) + (-x) \times (5) =$
Now simplify:

$(-x)(-2x^2) + (-x) \times (4x) + (-x) \times (5) = 2x^3 - 4x^2 - 5x$

Multiplying Binomials

- A binomial is a polynomial that is the sum or the difference of two terms, each of which is a monomial.

- To multiply two binomials, use the "FOIL" method. (First–Out–In–Last)

$$(x + a)(x + b) = x \times x + x \times b + a \times x + a \times b = x^2 + bx + ax + ab$$

Examples:

Example 1. Multiply Binomials. $(x + 3)(x - 2) =$

Solution: Use "FOIL". (First–Out–In–Last):
$(x + 3)(x - 2) = x^2 - 2x + 3x - 6$
Then combine like terms: $x^2 - 2x + 3x - 6 = x^2 + x - 6$

Example 2. Multiply. $(x + 6)(x + 4) =$

Solution: Use "FOIL". (First–Out–In–Last):
$(x + 6)(x + 4) = x^2 + 4x + 6x + 24$
Then simplify: $x^2 + 4x + 6x + 24 = x^2 + 10x + 24$

Example 3. Multiply. $(x + 5)(x - 7) =$

Solution: Use "FOIL". (First–Out–In–Last):
$(x + 5)(x - 7) = x^2 - 7x + 5x - 35$
Then simplify: $x^2 - 7x + 5x - 35 = x^2 - 2x - 35$

Example 4. Multiply Binomials. $(x - 9)(x - 5) =$

Solution: Use "FOIL". (First–Out–In–Last):
$(x - 9)(x - 5) = x^2 - 5x - 9x + 45$
Then combine like terms: $x^2 - 5x - 9x + 45 = x^2 - 14x + 45$

Factoring Trinomials

To factor trinomials, you can use following methods:

- "FOIL": $(x + a)(x + b) = x^2 + (b + a)x + ab$

- "Difference of Squares":

$$a^2 - b^2 = (a + b)(a - b)$$
$$a^2 + 2ab + b^2 = (a + b)(a + b)$$
$$a^2 - 2ab + b^2 = (a - b)(a - b)$$

- "Reverse FOIL": $x^2 + (b + a)x + ab = (x + a)(x + b)$

Examples:

Example 1. Factor this trinomial. $x^2 - 2x - 8$

Solution: Break the expression into groups. You need to find two numbers that their product is -8 and their sum is -2. (remember "Reverse FOIL": $x^2 + (b + a)x + ab = (x + a)(x + b)$). Those two numbers are 2 and -4. Then: $x^2 - 2x - 8 = (x^2 + 2x) + (-4x - 8)$
Now factor out x from $x^2 + 2x$: $x(x + 2)$, and factor out -4 from
$-4x - 8$: $-4(x + 2)$; Then: $(x^2 + 2x) + (-4x - 8) = x(x + 2) - 4(x + 2)$
Now factor out like term: $(x + 2)$. Then: $(x + 2)(x - 4)$

Example 2. Factor this trinomial. $x^2 - 2x - 24$

Solution: Break the expression into groups: $(x^2 + 4x) + (-6x - 24)$
Now factor out x from $x^2 + 4x$: $x(x + 4)$, and factor out -6 from
$-6x - 24$: $-6(x + 4)$; Then: $(x + 4) - 6(x + 4)$, now factor out like term:
$(x + 4) \rightarrow x(x + 4) - 6(x + 4) = (x + 4)(x - 6)$

Chapter 10: Practices

✍ Simplify each polynomial.

1) $3(6x + 4) =$

2) $5(3x - 8) =$

3) $x(7x + 2) + 9x =$

4) $6x(x + 3) + 5x =$

5) $6x(3x + 1) - 5x =$

6) $x(3x - 4) + 3x^2 - 6 =$

7) $x^2 - 5 - 3x(x + 8) =$

8) $2x^2 + 7 - 6x(2x + 5) =$

✍ Add or subtract polynomials.

9) $(x^2 + 3) + (2x^2 - 4) =$

10) $(3x^2 - 6x) - (x^2 + 8x) =$

11) $(4x^3 - 3x^2) + (2x^3 - 5x^2) =$

12) $(6x^3 - 7x) - (5x^3 - 3x) =$

13) $(10x^3 + 4x^2) + (14x^2 - 8) =$

14) $(4x^3 - 9) - (3x^3 - 7x^2) =$

15) $(9x^3 + 3x) - (6x^3 - 4x) =$

16) $(7x^3 - 5x) - (3x^3 + 5x) =$

✍ Find the products. (Multiplying Monomials)

17) $3x^2 \times 8x^3 =$

18) $2x^4 \times 9x^3 =$

19) $-4a^4b \times 2ab^3 =$

20) $(-7x^3yz) \times (3xy^2z^4) =$

21) $-2a^5bc \times 6a^2b^4 =$

22) $9u^3t^2 \times (-2ut) =$

23) $12x^2z \times 3xy^3 =$

24) $11x^3z \times 5xy^5 =$

25) $-6a^3bc \times 5a^4b^3 =$

26) $-4x^6y^2 \times (-12xy) =$

✎ **Simplify each expression. (Multiplying and Dividing Monomials)**

27) $(7x^2y^3)(3x^4y^2) =$

28) $(6x^3y^2)(4x^4y^3) =$

29) $(10x^8y^5)(3x^5y^7) =$

30) $(15a^3b^2)(2a^3b^8) =$

31) $\dfrac{42x^4y^2}{6x^3y} =$

32) $\dfrac{49x^5y^6}{7x^2y} =$

33) $\dfrac{63x^{15}y^{10}}{9x^8y^6} =$

34) $\dfrac{35x^8y^{12}}{5x^4y^8} =$

✎ **Find each product. (Multiplying a Polynomial and a Monomial)**

35) $3x(5x - y) =$

36) $2x(4x + y) =$

37) $7x(x - 3y) =$

38) $x(2x^2 + 2x - 4) =$

39) $5x(3x^2 + 8x + 2) =$

40) $7x(2x^2 - 9x - 5) =$

✎ **Find each product. (Multiplying Binomials)**

41) $(x - 3)(x + 3) =$

42) $(x - 6)(x + 6) =$

43) $(x + 10)(x + 4) =$

44) $(x - 6)(x + 7) =$

45) $(x + 2)(x - 5) =$

46) $(x - 10)(x + 3) =$

✎ **Factor each trinomial.**

47) $x^2 + 6x + 8 =$

48) $x^2 + 3x - 10 =$

49) $x^2 + 2x - 48 =$

50) $x^2 - 10x + 80 =$

51) $2x^2 - 7x + 12 =$

52) $3x^2 - 10x + 3 =$

Chapter 10: Answers

1) $18x + 12$

2) $15x - 40$

3) $7x^2 + 11x$

4) $6x^2 + 23x$

5) $18x^2 + x$

6) $6x^2 - 4x - 6$

7) $-2x^2 - 24x - 5$

8) $-10x^2 - 30x + 7$

9) $3x^2 - 1$

10) $2x^2 - 14x$

11) $6x^3 - 8x^2$

12) $x^3 - 4x$

13) $10x^3 + 18x^2 - 8$

14) $x^3 + 7x^2 - 9$

15) $3x^3 + 7x$

16) $4x^3 - 10x$

17) $24x^5$

18) $18x^7$

19) $-8a^5b^4$

20) $-21x^4y^3z^5$

21) $-12a^7b^5c$

22) $-18u^4t^3$

23) $36x^3y^3z$

24) $55x^4y^5z$

25) $-30a^7b^4c$

26) $48x^7y^3$

27) $21x^6y^5$

28) $24x^7y^5$

29) $30x^{13}y^{12}$

30) $30a^6b^{10}$

31) $7xy$

32) $7x^3y^5$

33) $7x^7y^4$

34) $7x^4y^4$

35) $15x^2 - 3xy$

36) $8x^2 + 2xy$

37) $7x^2 - 21xy$

38) $2x^3 + 2x^2 - 4x$

39) $15x^3 + 40x^2 + 10x$

40) $14x^3 - 63x^2 - 35x$

41) $x^2 - 9$

42) $x^2 - 36$

43) $x^2 + 14x + 40$

44) $x^2 + x - 42$

45) $x^2 - 3x - 10$

46) $x^2 - 7x - 30$

47) $(x + 4)(x + 2)$

48) $(x + 5)(x - 2)$

49) $(x - 6)(x + 8)$

50) $(x - 8)(x - 2)$

51) $(2x - 4)(x - 3)$

52) $(3x - 1)(x - 3)$

11 Geometry and Solid Figures

Math topics that you'll learn in this chapter:

- ☑ The Pythagorean Theorem
- ☑ Complementary and Supplementary angles
- ☑ Parallel lines and Transversals
- ☑ Triangles
- ☑ Special Right Triangles
- ☑ Polygons
- ☑ Circles
- ☑ Trapezoids
- ☑ Cubes
- ☑ Rectangle Prisms
- ☑ Cylinder

The Pythagorean Theorem

- You can use the Pythagorean Theorem to find a missing side in a right triangle.

- In any right triangle: $a^2 + b^2 = c^2$

Examples:

Example 3. Right triangle ABC (not shown) has two legs of lengths 3 cm (AB) and 4 cm (AC). What is the length of the hypotenuse of the triangle (side BC)?

Solution: Use Pythagorean Theorem: $a^2 + b^2 = c^2$, $a = 3$, and $b = 4$
Then: $a^2 + b^2 = c^2 \rightarrow 3^2 + 4^2 = c^2 \rightarrow 9 + 16 = c^2 \rightarrow 25 = c^2 \rightarrow c = \sqrt{25} = 5$
The length of the hypotenuse is 5 cm.

Example 4. Find the hypotenuse of this triangle.

Solution: Use Pythagorean Theorem: $a^2 + b^2 = c^2$
Then: $a^2 + b^2 = c^2 \rightarrow 8^2 + 6^2 = c^2 \rightarrow 64 + 36 = c^2$
$c^2 = 100 \rightarrow c = \sqrt{100} = 10$

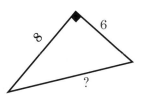

Example 5. Find the length of the missing side in this triangle.

Solution: Use Pythagorean Theorem: $a^2 + b^2 = c^2$
Then: $a^2 + b^2 = c^2 \rightarrow 12^2 + b^2 = 15^2 \rightarrow 144 + b^2 = 225 \rightarrow$
$\quad\quad\quad b^2 = 225 - 144 \rightarrow b^2 = 81 \rightarrow b = \sqrt{81} = 9$

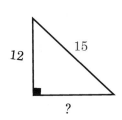

Complementary and Supplementary angles

- Two angles with a sum of 90 degrees are called complementary angles.

- Two angles with a sum of 180 degrees are Supplementary angles.

Examples:

Example 1. Find the missing angle.

Solution: Notice that the two angles form a right angle. This means that the angles are complementary, and their sum is 90.

Then: $18 + x = 90 \rightarrow x = 90^\circ - 18^\circ = 72^\circ$

The missing angle is 72 degrees. $x = 72^\circ$

Example 2. Angles Q and S are supplementary. What is the measure of angle Q if angle S is 35 degrees?

Solution: Q and S are supplementary $\rightarrow Q + S = 180 \rightarrow Q + 35 = 180 \rightarrow$

$$Q = 180 - 35 = 145$$

Parallel lines and Transversals

- When a line (transversal) intersects two parallel lines in the same plane, eight angles are formed. In the following diagram, a transversal intersects two parallel lines. Angles 1, 3, 5, and 7 are congruent. Angles 2, 4, 6, and 8 are also congruent.

- In the following diagram, the following angles are supplementary angles (their sum is 180):

  ❖ Angles 1 and 8

  ❖ Angles 2 and 7

  ❖ Angles 3 and 6

  ❖ Angles 4 and 5

Example:

Example 1. In the following diagram, two parallel lines are cut by a transversal. What is the value of x?

Solution: The two angles $3x - 15$ and $2x + 7$ are equivalent.

That is: $3x - 15 = 2x + 7$

Now, solve for x:

$3x - 15 + 15 = 2x + 7 + 15$

$\rightarrow 3x = 2x + 22 \rightarrow 3x - 2x = 2x + 22 - 2x$

$\rightarrow x = 22$

Triangles

- In any triangle, the sum of all angles is 180 degrees.

- Area of a triangle $= \frac{1}{2} (base \times height)$

Examples:

What is the area of the following triangles?

Example 1.

Solution: Use the area formula:

Area $= \frac{1}{2} (base \times height)$

$base = 14$ and $height = 10$

Area $= \frac{1}{2} (14 \times 10) = \frac{1}{2} (140) = 70$

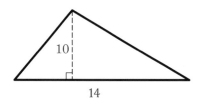

Example 2.

Solution: Use the area formula:

Area $= \frac{1}{2} (base \times height)$

$base = 16$ and $height = 8$; Area $= \frac{1}{2} (16 \times 8) = \frac{128}{2} = 64$

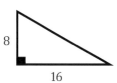

Example 3. What is the missing angle in this triangle?

Solution:

In any triangle, the sum of all angles is 180 degrees.

Let x be the missing angle.

Then: $55 + 80 + x = 180$;

$\rightarrow 135 + x = 180 \rightarrow x = 180 - 135 = 45$

The missing angle is 45 degrees.

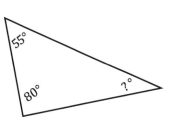

Special Right Triangles

- A special right triangle is a triangle whose sides are in a particular ratio. Two special right triangles are $45° - 45° - 90°$ and $30° - 60° - 90°$ triangles.

- In a special $45° - 45° - 90°$ triangle, the three angles are $45°$, $45°$ and $90°$. The lengths of the sides of this triangle are in the ratio of $1 : 1 : \sqrt{2}$.

- In a special triangle $30° - 60° - 90°$, the three angles are $30° - 60° - 90°$. The lengths of this triangle are in the ratio of $1 : \sqrt{3} : 2$.

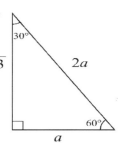

Examples:

Example 1. Find the length of the hypotenuse of a right triangle if the length of the other two sides are both 4 inches.

Solution: this is a right triangle with two equal sides. Therefore, it must be a $45° - 45° - 90°$ triangle. Two equivalent sides are 4 inches. The ratio of sides: $x : x : x\sqrt{2}$

The length of the hypotenuse is $4\sqrt{2}$ inches. $x : x : x\sqrt{2} \rightarrow 4 : 4 : 4\sqrt{2}$

Example 2. The length of the hypotenuse of a triangle is 6 inches. What are the lengths of the other two sides if one angle of the triangle is $30°$?

Solution: The hypotenuse is 6 inches and the triangle is a $30° - 60° - 90°$ triangle.

Then, one side of the triangle is 3 (it's half the side of the hypotenuse) and the other side is $3\sqrt{3}$. (it's the smallest side times $\sqrt{3}$)

$x : x\sqrt{3} : 2x \rightarrow x = 3 \rightarrow x : x\sqrt{3} : 2x = 3 : 3\sqrt{3} : 6$

Polygons

- The perimeter of a square = $4 \times side = 4s$

- The perimeter of a rectangle= $2(width + length)$

- The perimeter of trapezoid= $a + b + c + d$

- The perimeter of a regular hexagon = $6a$

- The perimeter of a parallelogram = $2(l + w)$

Examples:

Example 1. Find the perimeter of following regular hexagon.

Solution: Since the hexagon is regular, all sides are equal.
Then: The perimeter of The hexagon = $6 \times (one\ side)$
The perimeter of The hexagon = $6 \times (one\ side) = 6 \times 8 = 48\ m$

Example 2. Find the perimeter of following trapezoid.

Solution: The perimeter of a trapezoid = $a + b + c + d$
The perimeter of the trapezoid = $7 + 8 + 8 + 10 = 33\ ft$

bit.ly/3nFNiGi

Find more at

Circles

- In a circle, variable r is usually used for the radius and d for diameter.

- *Area of a circle* $= \pi r^2$ (π is about 3.14)

- *Circumference of a circle* $= 2\pi r$

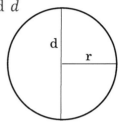

Examples:

Example 1. Find the area of this circle.

Solution:

Use area formula: $Area = \pi r^2$

$r = 6\ in \rightarrow Area = \pi(6)^2 = 36\pi$, $\pi = 3.14$

Then: $Area = 36 \times 3.14 = 113.04\ in^2$

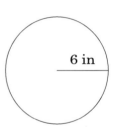

Example 2. Find the Circumference of this circle.

Solution:

Use Circumference formula: $Circumference = 2\pi r$

$r = 8\ cm \rightarrow Circumference = 2\pi(8) = 16\pi$

$\pi = 3.14$ Then: $Circumference = 16 \times 3.14 = 50.24\ cm$

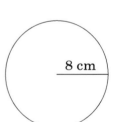

Example 3. Find the area of the circle.

Solution:

Use area formula: $Area = \pi r^2$,

$r = 9\ in$ then: $Area = \pi(9)^2 = 81\pi$, $\pi = 3.14$

Then: $Area = 81 \times 3.14 = 254.34\ in^2$

Trapezoids

- A quadrilateral with at least one pair of parallel sides is a trapezoid.

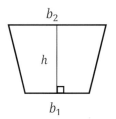

- Area of a trapezoid $= \frac{1}{2}h(b_1 + b_2)$

Examples:

Example 1. Calculate the area of this trapezoid.

Solution:

Use area formula: A $= \frac{1}{2}h(b_1 + b_2)$

$b_1 = 6 \, cm$, $b_2 = 10 \, cm$ and $h = 12 \, cm$

Then: A $= \frac{1}{2}(12)(10 + 6) = 6(16) = 96 \, cm^2$

Example 2. Calculate the area of this trapezoid.

Solution:

Use area formula: A $= \frac{1}{2}h(b_1 + b_2)$

$b_1 = 10 \, cm$, $b_2 = 18 \, cm$ and $h = 14 \, cm$

Then: A $= \frac{1}{2}(14)(10 + 18) = 7(28) = 196 \, cm^2$

Cubes

- A cube is a three-dimensional solid object bounded by six square sides.

- Volume is the measure of the amount of space inside of a solid figure, like a cube, ball, cylinder or pyramid.

- The volume of a cube = $(one\ side)^3$

- The surface area of a cube = $6 \times (one\ side)^2$

Examples:

Example 1. Find the volume and surface area of this cube.

Solution: Use volume formula: $volume = (one\ side)^3$
Then: $volume = (one\ side)^3 = (3)^3 = 27\ cm^3$
Use surface area formula:
$surface\ area\ of\ cube: 6(one\ side)^2 = 6(3)^2 = 6(9) = 54\ cm^2$

Example 2. Find the volume and surface area of this cube.

Solution: Use volume formula: $volume = (one\ side)^3$
Then: $volume = (one\ side)^3 = (6)^3 = 216\ cm^3$
Use surface area formula:
$surface\ area\ of\ cube: 6(one\ side)^2 = 6(6)^2 = 6(36) = 216\ cm^2$

Example 3. Find the volume and surface area of this cube.

Solution: Use volume formula: $volume = (one\ side)^3$
Then: $volume = (one\ side)^3 = (8)^3 = 512\ m^3$
Use surface area formula:
$surface\ area\ of\ cube: 6(one\ side)^2 = 6(8)^2 = 6(64) = 384\ m^2$

bit.ly/2M6PfOI
Find more at

Rectangular Prisms

- A rectangular prism is a solid 3-dimensional object with six rectangular faces.

- The volume of a Rectangular prism = $Length \times Width \times Height$

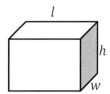

$Volume = l \times w \times h$

$Surface\ area = 2 \times (wh + lw + lh)$

Examples:

Example 1. Find the volume and surface area of this rectangular prism.

Solution: Use volume formula: $Volume = l \times w \times h$

Then: $Volume = 7 \times 5 \times 9 = 315\ m^3$

Use surface area formula: $Surface\ area = 2 \times (wh + lw + lh)$

Then: $Surface\ area = 2 \times \big((5 \times 9) + (7 \times 5) + (7 \times 9)\big)$

$= 2 \times (45 + 35 + 63) = 2 \times (143) = 286\ m^2$

Example 2. Find the volume and surface area of this rectangular prism.

Solution: Use volume formula: $Volume = l \times w \times h$

Then: $Volume = 9 \times 6 \times 12 = 648\ m^3$

Use surface area formula: $Surface\ area = 2 \times (wh + lw + lh)$

Then: $Surface\ area = 2 \times \big((6 \times 12) + (9 \times 6) + (9 \times 12)\big)$

$= 2 \times (72 + 54 + 108) = 2 \times (234) = 468\ m^2$

bit.ly/3nKm2GT
Find more at

Cylinder

- A cylinder is a solid geometric figure with straight parallel sides and a circular or oval cross-section.

- *Volume of a Cylinder* $= \pi(radius)^2 \times height$, $\pi \approx 3.14$

- *Surface area of a cylinder* $= 2\pi r^2 + 2\pi rh$

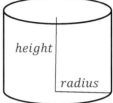

Examples:

Example 1. Find the volume and Surface area of the follow Cylinder.

Solution: Use volume formula:

$Volume = \pi(radius)^2 \times height$

Then: $Volume = \pi(4)^2 \times 10 = 16\pi \times 10 = 160\pi$

$\pi = 3.14$ then: $Volume = 160\pi = 160 \times 3.14 = 502.4 \ cm^3$

Use surface area formula: $Surface\ area = 2\pi r^2 + 2\pi rh$

Then: $2\pi(4)^2 + 2\pi(4)(10) = 2\pi(16) + 2\pi(40) = 32\pi + 80\pi = 112\pi$

$\pi = 3.14$ Then: $Surface\ area = 112 \times 3.14 = 351.68 \ cm^2$

Example 2. Find the volume and Surface area of the follow Cylinder.

Solution: Use volume formula:

$Volume = \pi(radius)^2 \times height$

Then: $Volume = \pi(5)^2 \times 8 = \pi 25 \times 8 = 200\pi$

$\pi = 3.14$ then: $Volume = 200\pi = 628 \ cm^3$

Use surface area formula: $Surface\ area = 2\pi r^2 + 2\pi rh$

Then: $= 2\pi(5)^2 + 2\pi(5)(8) = 2\pi(25) + 2\pi(40) = 50\pi + 80\pi = 130\pi$

$\pi = 3.14$ then: $Surface\ area = 130 \times 3.14 = 408.2 \ cm^2$

Chapter 11: Practices

✍ **Find the missing side?**

1)

2)

3)

4)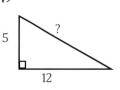

✍ **Find the measure of the unknown angle in each triangle.**

5)

6)

7)

8)

✍ **Find the area of each triangle.**

9)

10)

11)

12)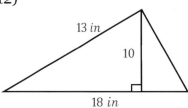

✍ **Find the perimeter or circumference of each shape.**

13)

14)

15)

16) *regular hexagon*

✎ Find the area of each trapezoid.

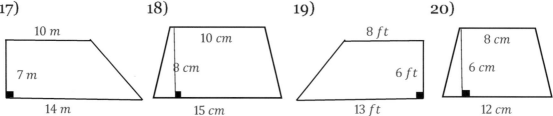

17)

10 m

7 m

14 m

18)

10 cm

8 cm

15 cm

19)

8 ft

6 ft

13 ft

20)

8 cm

6 cm

12 cm

✎ Find the volume of each cube.

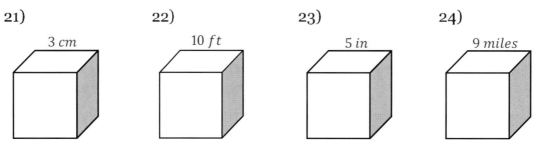

21)

3 cm

22)

10 ft

23)

5 in

24)

9 miles

✎ Find the volume of each Rectangular Prism.

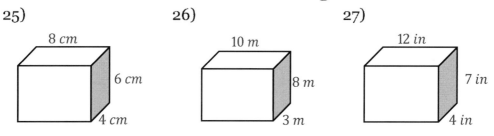

25)

8 cm

6 cm

4 cm

26)

10 m

8 m

3 m

27)

12 in

7 in

4 in

✎ Find the volume of each Cylinder. Round your answer to the nearest tenth. ($\pi = 3.14$)

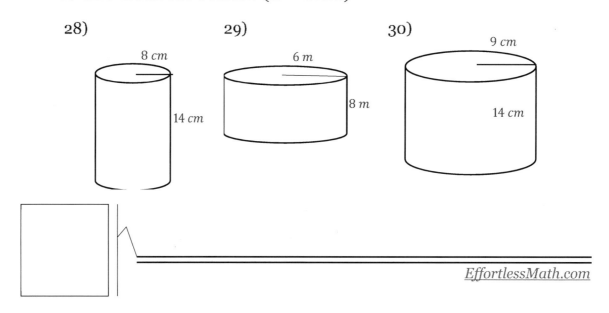

28)

8 cm

14 cm

29)

6 m

8 m

30)

9 cm

14 cm

Chapter 11: Answers

1) 4

2) 15

3) 6

4) 13

5) 50

6) 76

7) 84

8) 70

9) 30

10) 49.5

11) $64\ cm^2$

12) $90\ in^2$

13) $44\ cm$

14) $30\ ft$

15) $10\ \pi \approx 31.4\ in$

16) $24\ m$

17) $84\ m^2$

18) $100\ cm^2$

19) $63\ ft^2$

20) $60\ cm^2$

21) $27\ cm^3$

22) $1,000\ ft^3$

23) $125\ in^3$

24) $729\ mi^3$

25) $192\ cm^3$

26) $240\ m^3$

27) $336\ in^3$

28) $2,813.44\ cm^3$

29) $904.32\ m^3$

30) $3,560.76\ cm^3$

CHAPTER

12 Statistics

Math topics that you'll learn in this chapter:

☑ Mean, Median, Mode, and Range of the Given Data

☑ Pie Graph

☑ Probability Problems

☑ Permutations and Combinations

Mean, Median, Mode, and Range of the Given Data

- Mean: $\dfrac{sum\ of\ the\ data}{total\ number\ of\ data\ entires}$

- Mode: the value in the list that appears most often

- Median: is the middle number of a group of numbers arranged in order by size.

- Range: the difference of the largest value and smallest value in the list

Examples:

Example 1. What is the mode of these numbers? $5, 6, 8, 6, 8, 5, 3, 5$

Solution: Mode: the value in the list that appears most often.
Therefore, the mode is number 5. There are three number 5 in the data.

Example 2. What is the median of these numbers? $6, 11, 15, 10, 17, 20, 7$

Solution: Write the numbers in order: $6, 7, 10, 11, 15, 17, 20$
The median is the number in the middle. Therefore, the median is 11.

Example 3. What is the mean of these numbers? $7, 2, 3, 2, 4, 8, 7, 5$

Solution: Mean: $\dfrac{sum\ of\ the\ data}{total\ number\ of\ data\ entires} = \dfrac{7+2+3+2+4+8+7+5}{8} = \dfrac{38}{8} = 4.75$

Example 4. What is the range in this list? $3, 7, 12, 6, 15, 20, 8$

Solution: Range is the difference of the largest value and smallest value in the list. The largest value is 20 and the smallest value is 3.
Then: $20 - 3 = 17$

bit.ly/2KO86gg
Find more at

Pie Graph

- A Pie Chart is a circle chart divided into sectors, each sector represents the relative size of each value.

- Pie charts represent a snapshot of how a group is broken down into smaller pieces.

Example:

A library has 750 books that include Mathematics, Physics, Chemistry, English and History. Use the following graph to answer the questions.

Example 1. What is the number of Mathematics books?

Solution: Number of total books = 750
Percent of Mathematics books = 28% = 0.28
Then, the number of Mathematics books: $0.28 \times 750 = 210$

Example 2. What is the number of History books?

Solution: Number of total books = 750
Percent of History books = 12% = 0.12
Then: $0.12 \times 750 = 90$

Example 3. What is the number of Chemistry books?

Solution: Number of total books = 750
Percent of Chemistry books = 22% = 0.22
Then: $0.22 \times 750 = 165$

Probability Problems

- Probability is the likelihood of something happening in the future. It is expressed as a number between zero (can never happen) to 1 (will always happen).

- Probability can be expressed as a fraction, a decimal, or a percent.

- Probability formula: $Probability = \frac{number\ of\ desired\ outcomes}{number\ of\ total\ outcomes}$

Examples:

Example 1. Anita's trick–or–treat bag contains 10 pieces of chocolate, 16 suckers, 16 pieces of gum, 22 pieces of licorice. If she randomly pulls a piece of candy from her bag, what is the probability of her pulling out a piece of sucker?

Solution: Probability $= \frac{number\ of\ desired\ outcomes}{number\ of\ total\ outcomes}$

Probability of pulling out a piece of sucker $= \frac{16}{10 + 16 + 16 + 22} = \frac{16}{64} = \frac{1}{4}$

Example 2. A bag contains 20 balls: four green, five black, eight blue, a brown, a red and one white. If 19 balls are removed from the bag at random, what is the probability that a brown ball has been removed?

Solution: If 19 balls are removed from the bag at random, there will be one ball in the bag. The probability of choosing a brown ball is 1 out of 20. Therefore, the probability of not choosing a brown ball is 19 out of 20 and the probability of having not a brown ball after removing 19 balls is the same. The answer is: $\frac{19}{20}$

Permutations and Combinations

Factorials are products, indicated by an exclamation mark. For example, $4! = 4 \times 3 \times 2 \times 1$ (Remember that $0!$ is defined to be equal to 1)

- **Permutations:** The number of ways to choose a sample of k elements from a set of n distinct objects where order does matter, and replacements are not allowed. For a permutation problem, use this formula:

$$_n\mathrm{P}_k = \frac{n!}{(n-k)!}$$

- **Combination:** The number of ways to choose a sample of r elements from a set of n distinct objects where order does not matter, and replacements are not allowed. For a combination problem, use this formula:

$$_n\mathrm{C}_r = \frac{n!}{r!\,(n-r)!}$$

Examples:

Example 1. How many ways can the first and second place be awarded to 7 people?

Solution: Since the order matters, (the first and second place are different!) we need to use permutation formula where n is 7 and k is 2. Then: $\frac{n!}{(n-k)!} = \frac{7!}{(7-2)!} = \frac{7!}{5!} = \frac{7\times6\times5!}{5!}$, remove $5!$ from both sides of the fraction. Then: $\frac{7\times6\times5!}{5!} = 7 \times 6 = 42$

Example 2. How many ways can we pick a team of 3 people from a group of 8?

Solution: Since the order doesn't matter, we need to use a combination formula where n is 8 and r is 3.
Then: $\frac{n!}{r!\,(n-r)!} = \frac{8!}{3!\,(8-3)!} = \frac{8!}{3!\,(5)!} = \frac{8\times7\times6\times5!}{3!\,(5)!} = \frac{8\times7\times6}{3\times2\times1} = \frac{336}{6} = 56$

Chapter 12: Practices

✍ Find the values of the Given Data.

1) $6, 11, 5, 3, 6$

Mode: _____   Range: _____

Mean: _____   Median: _____

2) $4, 9, 1, 9, 6, 7$

Mode: _____   Range: _____

Mean: _____   Median: _____

3) $10, 3, 6, 10, 4, 15$

Mode: _____   Range: _____

Mean: _____   Median: _____

4) $12, 4, 8, 9, 3, 12, 15$

Mode: _____   Range: _____

Mean: _____   Median: _____

✍ The circle graph below shows all Bob's expenses for last month. Bob spent $790 on his Rent last month.

5) How much did Bob's total expenses last month? _____

6) How much did Bob spend for foods last month? _____

7) How much did Bob spend for his bills last month? _____

8) How much did Bob spend on his car last month? _____

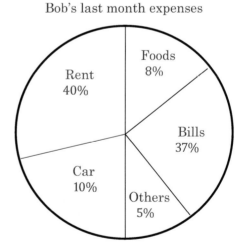

Bob's last month expenses

Rent 40%

Foods 8%

Bills 37%

Car 10%

Others 5%

✍ Solve.

9) Bag A contains 8 red marbles and 6 green marbles. Bag B contains 5 black marbles and 7 orange marbles. What is the probability of selecting a green marble at random from bag A? What is the probability of selecting a black marble at random from Bag B?

_____   _____

✍ Solve.

10) Susan is baking cookies. She uses sugar, flour, butter, and eggs. How many different orders of ingredients can she try? _____

11) Jason is planning for his vacation. He wants to go to museum, go to the beach, and play volleyball. How many different ways of ordering are there for him? _____

12) In how many ways can a team of 6 basketball players choose a captain and co-captain? _____

13) How many ways can you give 5 balls to your 8 friends? _____

14) A professor is going to arrange her 5 students in a straight line. In how many ways can she do this? _____

15) In how many ways can a teacher chooses 12 out of 15 students? _____

Chapter 12: Answers

1) Mode: 6, Range: 8, Mean: 6.2, Median: 6

2) Mode: 9, Range:8, Mean: 6, Median: 6.5

3) Mode: 10, Range: 12, Mean: 8, Median: 8

4) Mode: 12, Range: 12, Mean: 9, Median: 9

5) $1,975

6) $158

7) $730.75

8) $197.50

9) $\frac{3}{7}, \frac{5}{12}$

10) 24

11) 6

12) 30 (it's a permutation problem)

13) 56 (it's a combination problem)

14) 120

15) 455 (it's a combination problem)

CHAPTER

13 Quadratic

Math topics that you'll learn in this chapter:

☑ Solving a Quadratic Equation

☑ Graphing Quadratic Functions

☑ Solving Quadratic Inequalities

☑ Graphing Quadratic Inequalities

Solving a Quadratic Equation

- Write the equation in the form of: $ax^2 + bx + c = 0$

- Factorize the quadratic, set each factor equal to zero and solve.

- Use quadratic formula if you couldn't factorize the quadratic.

- Quadratic formula: $x = \frac{-b \pm \sqrt{b^2 - 4ac}}{2a}$

Examples:

Find the solutions of each quadratic function.

Example 1. $x^2 + 7x + 12 = 0$

Solution: Factor the quadratic by grouping. We need to find two numbers whose sum is 7 (from $7x$) and whose product is 12. Those numbers are 3 and 4. Then: $x^2 + 7x + 12 = 0 \rightarrow x^2 + 3x + 4x + 12 = 0 \rightarrow (x^2 + 3x) + (4x + 12) = 0$, Now, find common factors: $(x^2 + 3x) = x(x + 3)$ and $(4x + 12) = 3(x + 4)$. We have two expressions $(x^2 + 3x)$ and $(4x + 12)$ and their common factor is $(x + 3)$. Then: $(x^2 + 3x) + (4x + 12) = 0 \rightarrow x(x + 3) + 4(x + 3) = 0 \rightarrow (x + 3)(x + 4) = 0$.
The product of two expressions is 0. Then:
$(x + 3) = 0 \rightarrow x = -3$ or $(x + 4) = 0 \rightarrow x = -4$

Example 2. $x^2 + 5x + 6 = 0$

Solution: Use quadratic formula: $x_{1,2} = \frac{-b \pm \sqrt{b^2 - 4ac}}{2a}$, $a = 1, b = 5$ and $c = 6$

Then: $x = \frac{-5 \pm \sqrt{5^2 - 4 \times 1(6)}}{2(1)}$, $x_1 = \frac{-5 + \sqrt{5^2 - 4 \times 1(6)}}{2(1)} = -2$, $x_2 = \frac{-5 - \sqrt{5^2 - 4 \times 1(6)}}{2(1)} = -3$

Graphing Quadratic Functions

- Quadratic functions in vertex form: $y = a(x - h)^2 + k$ where (h, k) is the vertex of the function. The axis of symmetry is $x = h$

- Quadratic functions in standard form: $y = ax^2 + bx + c$ where $x = -\frac{b}{2a}$ is the value of x in the vertex of the function.

- To graph a quadratic function, first find the vertex, then substitute some values for x and solve for y. (Remember that the graph of a quadratic function is a U-shaped curve and it is called "parabola".)

Example:

Sketch the graph of $y = (x + 2)^2 - 3$

Solution: Quadratic functions in vertex form: $y = a(x - h)^2 + k$ and (h, k) is the vertex. Then, the vertex of $y = (x + 2)^2 - 3$ is $(-2, -3)$.

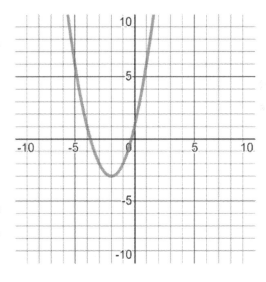

Substitute zero for x and solve for y:
$y = (0 + 2)^2 - 3 = 1$.
The y Intercept is $(0,1)$.

Now, you can simply graph the quadratic function. Notice that quadratic function is a U-shaped curve.

Solving Quadratic Inequalities

- A quadratic inequality is one that can be written in the standard form of $ax^2 + bx + c > 0$ (or substitute $<, \leq,$ or $\geq$ for $>$).

- Solving a quadratic inequality is like solving equations. We need to find the solutions (the zeroes).

- To solve quadratic inequalities, first find quadratic equations. Then choose a test value between zeroes. Finally, find interval(s), such as > 0 or < 0.

Examples:

Example 1. Solve quadratic inequality. $x^2 + x - 6 > 0$

Solution: First solve $x^2 + x - 6 = 0$ by factoring. Then: $x^2 + x - 6 = 0 \rightarrow (x-2)(x+3) = 0$. The product of two expressions is 0. Then: $(x-2) = 0 \rightarrow x = 2$ or $(x+3) = 0 \rightarrow x = -3$. Now, choose a value between 2 and -3. Let's choose 0. Then: $x = 0 \rightarrow x^2 + x - 6 > 0 \rightarrow (0)^2 + (0) - 6 > 0 \rightarrow -6 > 0$

-6 is not greater than 0. Therefore, all values between 2 and -3 are NOT the solution of this quadratic inequality. The solution is: $x > 2$ and $x < -3$. To represent the solution, we can use interval notation, in which solution sets are indicated with parentheses or brackets. The solutions $x > 2$ and $x < -3$ represented as: $(\infty, -3) \cup (2, \infty)$

Solution $x \geq 2$ represented as: $[2, \infty)$

Example 2. Solve quadratic inequality. $x^2 - 2x - 8 \geq 0$

Solution: First solve: $x^2 - 2x - 8 = 0$, Factor: $x^2 - 2x - 8 = 0 \rightarrow (x-4)(x+2) = 0$.

-2 and 4 are the solutions. Choose a point between -2 and 4. Let's choose 0. Then: $x = 0 \rightarrow x^2 - 2x - 8 \geq 0 \rightarrow (0)^2 - 2(0) - 8 \geq 0 \rightarrow -8 \geq 0$.

This is NOT true. So, the solution is: $x \leq -2$ or $x \geq 4$ (using interval notation the solution is: $(\infty, -2] \cup [4, \infty)$

Graphing Quadratic Inequalities

- A quadratic inequality is in the form

$y > ax^2 + bx + c$ (or substitute $<, \leq,$ or $\geq$ for $>$).

- To graph a quadratic inequality, start by graphing the quadratic parabola. Then fill in the region either inside or outside of it, depending on the inequality.

- Choose a testing point and check the solution section.

Example:

Sketch the graph of $y = 2x^2$

Solution: First, graph the quadratic $y = 2x^2$ Since the inequality sing is $>$, we need to use dash lines.

Now, choose a testing point inside the parabola. Let's choose $(0,2)$.

$y > 2x^2 \rightarrow 2 > 2(0)^2 \rightarrow 2 > 0$

This is true. So, inside the parabola is the solution section.

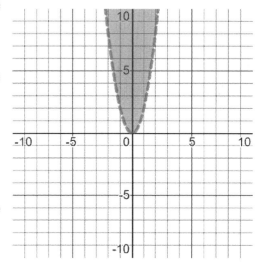

bit.ly/3b5XXWq

Chapter 13: Practices

✍️ **Solve each equation by factoring or using the quadratic formula.**

1) $x^2 - 4x - 32 = 0$

_____

2) $x^2 - 2x - 63 = 0$

_____

3) $x^2 + 17x + 72 = 0$

_____

4) $x^2 + 14x + 48 = 0$

_____

5) $x^2 + 5x - 24 = 0$

_____

6) $x^2 + 15x + 36 = 0$

_____

✍️ **Sketch the graph of each function.**

7) $y = (x + 1)^2 - 2$

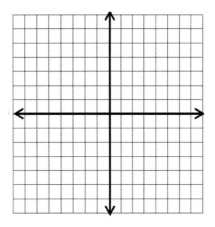

8) $y = (x - 1)^2 + 3$

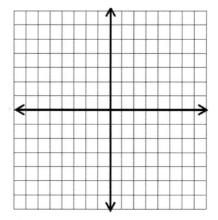

✍ **Solve each quadratic inequality.**

9) $x^2 - 4 < 0$

_____

10) $x^2 - 9 > 0$

_____

11) $x^2 - 5x - 6 < 0$

_____

12) $x^2 + 8x - 20 > 0$

_____

13) $x^2 + 10x - 24 \geq 0$

_____

14) $x^2 + 17x + 72 \leq 0$

_____

✍ **Sketch the graph of each quadratic inequality.**

15) $y < -2x^2$

16) $y > 3x^2$

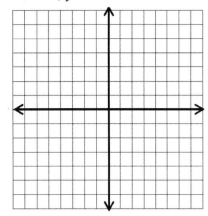

Chapter 13: Answers

1) $x^2 - 4x - 32 = 0$

$x = 8, x = -4$

2) $x^2 - 2x - 63 = 0$

$x = 9, x = -7$

3) $x^2 + 17x + 72 = 0$

$x = -9, x = -8$

4) $x^2 + 14x + 48 = 0$

$x = -6, x = -8$

5) $x^2 + 5x - 24 = 0$

$x = 3, x = -8$

6) $x^2 + 15x + 36 = 0$

$x = -12, x = -3$

7) $y = (x + 1)^2 - 2$

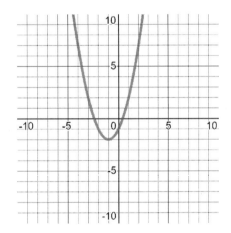

8) $y = (x - 1)^2 + 3$

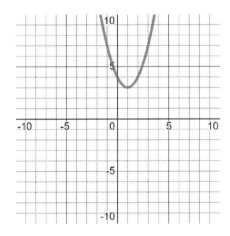

9) $x^2 - 4 < 0$

$-2 < x < 2$

10) $x^2 - 9 > 0$

$-3 < x < 3$

11) $x^2 - 5x - 6 < 0$

$-1 < x < 6$

12) $x^2 + 8x - 20 > 0$

$x < -10 \ or \ x > 2$

13) $x^2 + 10x - 24 \geq 0$

$x \leq -12 \; or \; x \geq 2$

14) $x^2 + 17x + 72 \leq 0$

$-9 \leq x \leq -8$

15) $y < -2x^2$

16) $y > 3x^2$

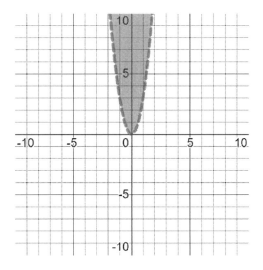

Time to Test

Time to refine your skill with a practice examination

Take practice ISEE Upper Level Math Tests to simulate the test day experience. After you've finished, score your tests using the answer keys.

Before You Start

- You'll need a pencil and a timer to take the test.

- For each question, there are four possible answers. Choose which one is best.

- After you've finished the test, review the answer key to see where you went wrong.

- Use the answer sheet provided to record your answers. (You can cut it out or photocopy it)

- You will receive 1 point for every correct answer, and you will lose $\frac{1}{4}$ point for each incorrect answer. There is no penalty for skipping a question.

Calculators are NOT permitted for the ISEE Upper Level Test

ISEE Upper Level Math Practice Test 1

2023 - 2023

Two Parts

Total number of questions: 84

Part 1 (Calculator): 37 questions

Part 2 (Calculator): 47 questions

Total time for two parts: 75 Minutes

ISEE Upper Level Practice Test Answer Sheets

Remove (or photocopy) this answer sheet and use it to complete the practice test.

ISEE Upper Level Practice Test 1			
Quantitative Reasoning		**Mathematics Achievement**	

Quantitative Reasoning

1 Ⓐ Ⓑ Ⓒ Ⓓ   25 Ⓐ Ⓑ Ⓒ Ⓓ
2 Ⓐ Ⓑ Ⓒ Ⓓ   26 Ⓐ Ⓑ Ⓒ Ⓓ
3 Ⓐ Ⓑ Ⓒ Ⓓ   27 Ⓐ Ⓑ Ⓒ Ⓓ
4 Ⓐ Ⓑ Ⓒ Ⓓ   28 Ⓐ Ⓑ Ⓒ Ⓓ
5 Ⓐ Ⓑ Ⓒ Ⓓ   29 Ⓐ Ⓑ Ⓒ Ⓓ
6 Ⓐ Ⓑ Ⓒ Ⓓ   30 Ⓐ Ⓑ Ⓒ Ⓓ
7 Ⓐ Ⓑ Ⓒ Ⓓ   31 Ⓐ Ⓑ Ⓒ Ⓓ
8 Ⓐ Ⓑ Ⓒ Ⓓ   32 Ⓐ Ⓑ Ⓒ Ⓓ
9 Ⓐ Ⓑ Ⓒ Ⓓ   33 Ⓐ Ⓑ Ⓒ Ⓓ
10 Ⓐ Ⓑ Ⓒ Ⓓ   34 Ⓐ Ⓑ Ⓒ Ⓓ
11 Ⓐ Ⓑ Ⓒ Ⓓ   35 Ⓐ Ⓑ Ⓒ Ⓓ
12 Ⓐ Ⓑ Ⓒ Ⓓ   36 Ⓐ Ⓑ Ⓒ Ⓓ
13 Ⓐ Ⓑ Ⓒ Ⓓ   37 Ⓐ Ⓑ Ⓒ Ⓓ
14 Ⓐ Ⓑ Ⓒ Ⓓ
15 Ⓐ Ⓑ Ⓒ Ⓓ
16 Ⓐ Ⓑ Ⓒ Ⓓ
17 Ⓐ Ⓑ Ⓒ Ⓓ
18 Ⓐ Ⓑ Ⓒ Ⓓ
19 Ⓐ Ⓑ Ⓒ Ⓓ
20 Ⓐ Ⓑ Ⓒ Ⓓ
21 Ⓐ Ⓑ Ⓒ Ⓓ
22 Ⓐ Ⓑ Ⓒ Ⓓ
23 Ⓐ Ⓑ Ⓒ Ⓓ
24 Ⓐ Ⓑ Ⓒ Ⓓ

Mathematics Achievement

1 Ⓐ Ⓑ Ⓒ Ⓓ   25 Ⓐ Ⓑ Ⓒ Ⓓ
2 Ⓐ Ⓑ Ⓒ Ⓓ   26 Ⓐ Ⓑ Ⓒ Ⓓ
3 Ⓐ Ⓑ Ⓒ Ⓓ   27 Ⓐ Ⓑ Ⓒ Ⓓ
4 Ⓐ Ⓑ Ⓒ Ⓓ   28 Ⓐ Ⓑ Ⓒ Ⓓ
5 Ⓐ Ⓑ Ⓒ Ⓓ   29 Ⓐ Ⓑ Ⓒ Ⓓ
6 Ⓐ Ⓑ Ⓒ Ⓓ   30 Ⓐ Ⓑ Ⓒ Ⓓ
7 Ⓐ Ⓑ Ⓒ Ⓓ   31 Ⓐ Ⓑ Ⓒ Ⓓ
8 Ⓐ Ⓑ Ⓒ Ⓓ   32 Ⓐ Ⓑ Ⓒ Ⓓ
9 Ⓐ Ⓑ Ⓒ Ⓓ   33 Ⓐ Ⓑ Ⓒ Ⓓ
10 Ⓐ Ⓑ Ⓒ Ⓓ   34 Ⓐ Ⓑ Ⓒ Ⓓ
11 Ⓐ Ⓑ Ⓒ Ⓓ   35 Ⓐ Ⓑ Ⓒ Ⓓ
12 Ⓐ Ⓑ Ⓒ Ⓓ   36 Ⓐ Ⓑ Ⓒ Ⓓ
13 Ⓐ Ⓑ Ⓒ Ⓓ   37 Ⓐ Ⓑ Ⓒ Ⓓ
14 Ⓐ Ⓑ Ⓒ Ⓓ   38 Ⓐ Ⓑ Ⓒ Ⓓ
15 Ⓐ Ⓑ Ⓒ Ⓓ   39 Ⓐ Ⓑ Ⓒ Ⓓ
16 Ⓐ Ⓑ Ⓒ Ⓓ   40 Ⓐ Ⓑ Ⓒ Ⓓ
17 Ⓐ Ⓑ Ⓒ Ⓓ   41 Ⓐ Ⓑ Ⓒ Ⓓ
18 Ⓐ Ⓑ Ⓒ Ⓓ   42 Ⓐ Ⓑ Ⓒ Ⓓ
19 Ⓐ Ⓑ Ⓒ Ⓓ   43 Ⓐ Ⓑ Ⓒ Ⓓ
20 Ⓐ Ⓑ Ⓒ Ⓓ   44 Ⓐ Ⓑ Ⓒ Ⓓ
21 Ⓐ Ⓑ Ⓒ Ⓓ   45 Ⓐ Ⓑ Ⓒ Ⓓ
22 Ⓐ Ⓑ Ⓒ Ⓓ   46 Ⓐ Ⓑ Ⓒ Ⓓ
23 Ⓐ Ⓑ Ⓒ Ⓓ   47 Ⓐ Ⓑ Ⓒ Ⓓ
24 Ⓐ Ⓑ Ⓒ Ⓓ

ISEE Upper Level
Practice Test 1

Part 1 (Quantitative Reasoning)

- o **37 questions**
- o **Total time for this section:** 35 Minutes
- o **Calculators are not allowed at the test.**

1) What is the prime factorization of 560?

A. $2 \times 2 \times 5 \times 7$

B. $2 \times 2 \times 2 \times 2 \times 5 \times 7$

C. 2×7

D. $2 \times 2 \times 2 \times 5 \times 7$

2) A basket contains 20 balls and the average weight of each of these balls is 25 g. The five heaviest balls have an average weight of 40 g each. If we remove the three heaviest balls from the basket, what is the average weight of the remaining balls?

A. 10 g

B. 20 g

C. 30 g

D. 35 g

3) How much greater is the value of $5x + 8$ than the value of $5x - 3$?

A. 7

B. 9

C. 11

D. 13

4) If 5 inches on a map represents an actual distance of 100 feet, then what actual distance does 18 inches on the map represent?

A. 18 feet

B. 100 feet

C. 250 feet

D. 360 feet

5) The circle graph below shows all Mr. Green's expenses for last month. If he spent $660 on his car, how much did he spend for his rent?

A. $700

B. $740

C. $780

D. $810

Mr. Green's monthly expenses

6) Alice drives from her house to work at an average speed of 55 miles per hour and she drives at an average speed of 62 miles per hour when she was returning home. What was her minimum speed on the round trip in miles per hour?

A. 55

B. 58.5

C. 62

D. Cannot be determined

7) The area of a circle is less than $64\,\pi$. Which of the following can be the circumference of the circle?

A. $12\,\pi$

B. $16\,\pi$

C. $24\,\pi$

D. $32\,\pi$

8) Oscar purchased a new hat that was on sale for $7.35. The original price was $12.65. What percentage discount was the sale price?

A. 4.2%

B. 40.5%

C. 42%

D. 45%

9) If $f(x) = x^2 + 5$, what is the smallest possible value of $f(x)$?

A. 0

B. 4

C. 5

D. 7

10) If the sum of the positive integers from 1 to n is 2,250, and the sum of the positive integers from $n + 1$ to $2n$ is 4,356, which of the following represents the sum of the positive integers from 1 to $2n$ inclusive?

A. 2,106

B. 4,356

C. 6,000

D. 6,606

11) Which of the following statements is correct, according to the graph below?

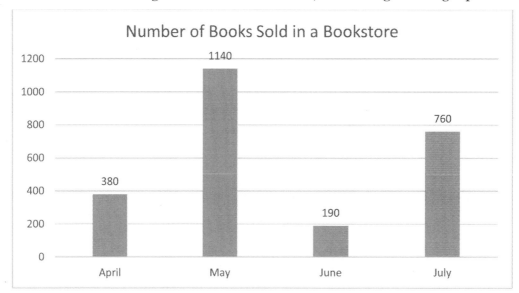

A. Number of books sold in April was twice the number of books sold in July.

B. Number of books sold in July was less than half the number of books sold in May.

C. Number of books sold in June was half the number of books sold in April.

D. Number of books sold in July was equal to the number of books sold in April plus the number of books sold in June.

12) List A consists of the numbers $\{1, 3, 8, 10, 15\}$, and list B consists of the numbers $\{4, 6, 12, 14, 17\}$.

If the two lists are combined, what is the median of the combined list?

A. 6

B. 8

C. 9

D. 10

13) If Jim adds 100 stamps to his current stamp collection, the total number of stamps will be equal to $\frac{6}{5}$ the current number of stamps. If Jim adds 50% more stamps to the current collection, how many stamps will be in the collection?

A. 150

B. 300

C. 600

D. 750

14) A bag contains 18 balls: two green, five black, eight blue, a brown, a red and one white. If 17 balls are removed from the bag at random, what is the probability that a brown ball has been removed?

A. $\frac{1}{9}$

B. $\frac{1}{6}$

C. $\frac{16}{17}$

D. $\frac{17}{18}$

15) If $x + y = 8$ and $x - y = 5$ then what is the value of $(x^2 - y^2)$?

A. 23

B. 40

C. 65

D. 90

16) What's The ratio of boys and girls in a class is $4:7$. If there are 44 students in the class, how many more boys should be enrolled to make the ratio $1:1$?

A. 8

B. 10

C. 12

D. 16

17) The area of rectangle $ABCD$ is 196 square inches. If the length of the rectangle is four times the width, what is the perimeter of rectangle $ABCD$?

A. 56 inches

B. 70 inches

C. 84 inches

D. 90 inches

18) The sum of 8 numbers is greater than 160 and less than 240. Which of the following could be the average (arithmetic mean) of the numbers?

A. 20

B. 25

C. 40

D. 45

19) Which of the following expressions gives the value of b in terms of a, c, and z from the following equation?

$$a = [\frac{cz}{b}]^2$$

A. $b = ac^2z^2$

B. $b = \frac{cz}{\sqrt{a}}$

C. $b = \frac{\sqrt{a}}{cz}$

D. $b = [\frac{cz}{a}]^2$

20) Triangle *ABC* is similar to triangle *ADE*. What is the length of side *EC*?

A. 4

B. 9

C. 18

D. 45

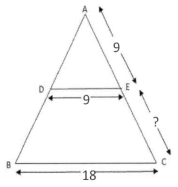

21) A gas tank can hold 25 gallons when it is $\frac{2}{5}$ full. How many gallons does it contain when it is full?

A. 125

B. 62.5

C. 50

D. 10

Quantitative Comparisons

Direction: Questions 22 to 37 are Quantitative Comparisons Questions. Using the information provided in each question, compare the quantity in column A to the quantity in Column B. Choose on your answer sheet grid

A. if the quantity in Column A is greater

B. if the quantity in Column B is greater

C. if the two quantities are equal

D. if the relationship cannot be determined from the information given

22)

Column A	Column B
The average of 15, 25, and 27	20

23)

Column A	Column B
$11 \times 675 \times 24$	$18 \times 675 \times 17$

24) x is an integer

Column A	Column B
x	$\dfrac{x}{-2}$

25)

Column A	Column B
The greatest value of x in	The greatest value of x in
$6\,|2x - 4| = 6$	$6\,|2x + 4| = 6$

26) x is an integer

Column A	Column B
$(x)^3(x)^4$	$(x^3)^4$

27)

Column A	Column B
The probability that	The probability that
event x will occur.	event x will not occur.

28)

Column A	Column B
2^2	$\sqrt[3]{64}$

29)

Column A	Column B
8	$(59)^{\frac{1}{2}}$

30) The selling price of a sport jacket including 25% discount is $51.

Column A	Column B
Original price of the sport jacket	$67

31)

Column A	Column B
$(0.69)^{34}$	$(0.69)^{33}$

32)

Column A	Column B
The probability of rolling a 6 on a die and getting heads on a coin toss.	The probability of rolling an even number on a die and picking a spade from a deck of 52 cards.

33)

Column A	Column B
$(\frac{1}{5})^2$	5^{-2}

34) $x + 2 > 5x$

Column A	Column B
x	-1

35)

Column A	Column B
$0.41	Sum of one quarter, two nickels, and three pennies

36) x is an odd integer, and y is an even integer. In a certain game an odd number is considered greater than an even number.

Column A	Column B
$(x + y)^2 - y$	$(y)(x - y)$

37) $x^2 - 5x - 8 = 6$

Column A	Column B
x	0

STOP: This is the End of Section 1 of test 1.

ISEE Upper Level

Practice Test 1

Part 2 (Mathematics Achievement)

- o **47 questions**
- o **Total time for this section:** 40 Minutes
- o **Calculators are not allowed at the test.**

1) $\frac{1}{6b^2} + \frac{1}{6b} = \frac{1}{b^2}$, then $b = ?$

A. $-\frac{16}{15}$

B. 5

C. $-\frac{15}{16}$

D. 8

2) If $\frac{|3+x|}{7} \leq 5$, then which of the following is correct?

A. $-38 \leq x \leq 35$

B. $-38 \leq x \leq 32$

C. $-32 \leq x \leq 38$

D. $-32 \leq x \leq 32$

3) The cost, in thousands of dollars, of producing x thousands of textbooks is $C(x) = x^2 + 2x$. The revenue, also in thousands of dollars, is $R(x) = 40x$. find the profit or loss if 30 textbooks are produced. ($profit = revenue - cost$)

A. $2,160 $profit$

B. $240 $profit$

C. $2,160 $loss$

D. $240 $loss$

4) Ella (E) is 4 years older than her friend Ava (A) who is 3 years younger than her sister Sofia (S). If E, A and S denote their ages, which one of the following represents the given information?

A. $\begin{cases} E = A + 4 \\ S = A - 3 \end{cases}$

B. $\begin{cases} E = A + 4 \\ A = S + 3 \end{cases}$

C. $\begin{cases} A = E + 4 \\ S = A - 3 \end{cases}$

D. $\begin{cases} E = A + 4 \\ A = S - 3 \end{cases}$

5) 5 less than twice a positive integer is 83. What is the integer?

A. 39

B. 41

C. 42

D. 44

6) Which of the following points lies on the line $4x + 6y = 14$?

A. $(2, 1)$

B. $(-1, 2)$

C. $(-2, 2)$

D. $(2, 2)$

7) An angle is equal to one fifth of its supplement. What is the measure of that angle?

A. $20°$

B. $30°$

C. $45°$

D. $60°$

8) 1.2 is what percent of 24?

A. 1.2

B. 5

C. 12

D. 24

9) Right triangle ABC has two legs of lengths $6\ cm$ (AB) and $8\ cm$ (AC). What is the length of the third side (BC)?

A. $4\ cm$

B. $6\ cm$

C. $8\ cm$

D. $10\ cm$

10) Simplify $6x^2y^3(2x^2y)^3 =$

A. $12x^4y^6$

B. $12x^8y^6$

C. $48x^4y^6$

D. $48x^8y^6$

11) Which is the longest time?

A. 23 *hours*

B. 1520 *minutes*

C. 2 *days*

D. 4200 *seconds*

12) Write 523 in expanded form, using exponents.

A. $(5 \times 10^3) + (2 \times 10^2) + (3 \times 10)$

B. $(5 \times 10^2) + (2 \times 10^1) - 5$

C. $(5 \times 10^2) + (2 \times 10^1) + 3$

D. $(5 \times 10^1) + (2 \times 10^2) + 3$

13) A company pays its writer $4 for every 400 words written. How much will a writer earn for an article with 960 words?

A. $11

B. $5.6

C. $9.6

D. $10.7

14) A circular logo is enlarged to fit the lid of a jar. The new diameter is 30% larger than the original. By what percentage has the area of the logo increased?

A. 20%

B. 30%

C. 69%

D. 75%

15) A circle has a diameter of 8 inches. What is its approximate circumference?

A. 6.28 inches

B. 25.12 inches

C. 34.85 inches

D. 35.12 inches

16) What is the area of an isosceles right triangle with hypotenuse that measures 6 cm?

A. 9 cm^2

B. 18 cm^2

C. 3 $\sqrt{2}$ cm^2

D. 36 cm^2

17) What's the area of the non-shaded part of the following figure?

A. 192

B. 152

C. 40

D. 42

18) 79.22 ÷ 0.05 = ?

A. 15.844

B. 1,584.4

C. 158.44

D. 1.5844

19) A bread recipe calls for $3\frac{1}{3}$ cups of flour. If you only have $2\frac{5}{6}$ cups, how much more flour is needed?

A. 1

B. $\frac{1}{2}$

C. 2

D. $\frac{5}{6}$

20) The equation of a line is given as: $y = 5x - 3$. Which of the following points does not lie on the line?

A. $(1, 2)$

B. $(-2, -13)$

C. $(3, 18)$

D. $(2, 7)$

21) The drivers at G & G trucking must report the mileage on their trucks each week. The mileage reading of Ed's vehicle was 40,907 at the beginning of one week, and 41,053 at the end of the same week. What was the total number of miles driven by Ed that week?

A. 46 $MILES$

B. 145 $MILES$

C. 146 $MILES$

D. 1,046 $MILES$

22) What is the maximum value for y if $y = -(x - 2)^2 + 6$?

A. -6

B. -2

C. 2

D. 6

23) What is the solution of the following system of equations?

$$\begin{cases} -2x - y = -9 \\ 5x - 2y = 18 \end{cases}$$

A. $(-1, 2)$

B. $(4, 1)$

C. $(1, 4)$

D. $(4, -2)$

24) What is the area of an isosceles right triangle that has one leg that measures 6 cm?

A. 18 cm^2

B. 36 cm^2

C. $6\sqrt{2}$ cm^2

D. 72 cm^2

25) Which of the following is a factor of both $x^2 - 2x - 8$ and $x^2 - 6x + 8$?

A. $(x - 4)$

B. $(x + 4)$

C. $(x - 2)$

D. $(x + 2)$

26) $\frac{13}{25}$ is equal to:

A. 5.2

B. 0.52

C. 0.05

D. 0.5

27) If $x + y = 12$, what is the value of $8x + 8y$?

A. 192

B. 104

C. 96

D. 48

28) $\dfrac{\begin{array}{r} 37 \text{ hr. } 25 \text{ min.} \\ - 24 \text{ hr. } 38 \text{ min.} \end{array}}{\rule{2cm}{0.4pt}}$

A. $12 \, hr. \, 57 \, min.$

B. $12 \, hr. \, 47 \, min.$

C. $13 \, hr. \, 13 \, min.$

D. $13 \, hr. \, 57 \, min.$

29) A car uses 15 gallons of gas to travel 450 miles. How many miles per gallon does the car use?

A. 28 *miles per gallon*

B. 32 *miles per gallon*

C. 30 *miles per gallon*

D. 34 *miles per gallon*

30) What is the number of cubic feet of soil needed for a flower box 2 feet long, 8 inches wide, and 2 feet deep?

A. 32 *cubic feet*

B. 16 *cubic feet*

C. $\frac{8}{3}$ *cubic feet*

D. 2 *cubic feet*

31) What is the reciprocal of $\frac{x^3}{16}$?

A. $\frac{16}{x^3} - 1$

B. $\frac{48}{x^3}$

C. $\frac{16}{x^3} + 1$

D. $\frac{16}{x^3}$

32) Mario loaned Jett $1,200 at a yearly interest rate of 5%. After one year what is the interest owned on this loan?

A. $1,260

B. $120

C. $60

D. $30

33) Ellis just got hired for on-the-road sales and will travel about 2,500 miles a week during an 80-hour work week. If the time spent traveling is $\frac{3}{5}$ of his week, how many hours a week will he be on the road?

A. Ellis spends about 34 hours of his 80-hour work week on the road.

B. Ellis spends about 40 hours of his 80-hour work week on the road.

C. Ellis spends about 43 hours of his 80-hour work week on the road.

D. Ellis spends about 48 hours of his 80-hour work week on the road.

34) Given that $x = 0.6$ and $y = 6$, what is the value of $2x^2(y + 4)$?

A. 7.2

B. 8.2

C. 11.2

D. 13.2

35) aren is 9 years older than her sister Michelle, and Michelle is 4 years younger than her brother David. If the sum of their ages is 82, how old is Michelle?

A. 21

B. 23

C. 25

D. 29

36) Calculate the area of a parallelogram with a base of 2 feet and height of 2.4 feet.

A. 2.8 *square feet*

B. 4.2 *square feet*

C. 4.8 *square feet*

D. 8 *square feet*

37) A shirt costing $200 is discounted 25%. After a month, the shirt is discounted another 15%. Which of the following expressions can be used to find the selling price of the shirt?

A. $(200)(0.70)$

B. $(200) - 200(0.30)$

C. $(200)(0.15) - (200)(0.15)$

D. $(200)(0.75)(0.85)$

38) In a school, the ratio of number of boys to girls is $3:7$. If the number of boys is 180, what is the total number of students in the school?

A. 390

B. 500

C. 540

D. 600

39) A tree 32 feet tall casts a shadow 12 feet long. Jack is 6 feet tall. How long is Jack's shadow?

A. 2.25 ft

B. 4 ft

C. 4.25 ft

D. 8 ft

40) What is the area of the shaded region if the diameter of the bigger circle is 12 $inches$ and the diameter of the smaller circle is 8 inches.

A. 16 $\pi\ inch^2$

B. 20 $\pi\ inch^2$

C. 36 $\pi\ inch^2$

D. 80 $\pi\ inch^2$

41) What is the result of the expression?

$$\begin{vmatrix} 3 & 6 \\ -1 & -3 \\ -5 & -1 \end{vmatrix} + \begin{vmatrix} 0 & -1 \\ 6 & 0 \\ 2 & 3 \end{vmatrix}$$

A. $\begin{vmatrix} 0 & -1 \\ 6 & 0 \\ 2 & 3 \end{vmatrix}$

B. $\begin{vmatrix} 3 & 6 \\ -1 & -3 \\ -5 & -1 \end{vmatrix}$

C. $\begin{vmatrix} 3 & 5 \\ 5 & -3 \\ -3 & 2 \end{vmatrix}$

D. $\begin{vmatrix} 0 & -3 \\ -6 & 0 \\ -10 & -3 \end{vmatrix}$

42) How many square feet of tile is needed for a 18 feet × 18 feet room?

A. 72 $square\ feet$

B. 108 $square\ feet$

C. 324 $square\ feet$

D. 416 $square\ feet$

43) $(3x + 3)(x + 5) =$

A. $4x + 8$

B. $3x + 3x + 15$

C. $3x^2 + 18x + 15$

D. $3x^2 + 3$

44) If $x \blacksquare y = \sqrt{x^2 + y}$, what is the value of $5 \blacksquare 11$?

A. $\sqrt{126}$

B. 6

C. 4

D. 3

45) There are three equal tanks of water. If $\dfrac{2}{5}$ of a tank contains 200 liters of water, what is the capacity of the three tanks of water together?

A. 1,500 liters

B. 500 liters

C. 240 liters

D. 80 liters

46) The average weight of 18 girls in a class is 60 kg and the average weight of 32 boys in the same class is 62 kg. What is the average weight of all the 50 students in that class?

A. 60 kg

B. 61.28 kg

C. 61.68 kg

D. 61.9 kg

47) If x is 45% percent of 820, what is x?

A. 185

B. 369

C. 402

D. 720

STOP: This is the End of Section 2 of test 1.

ISEE Upper Level Math Practice Test 2

2023 - 2023

Two Parts

Total number of questions: 84

Part 1 (Calculator): 37 questions

Part 2 (Calculator): 47 questions

Total time for two parts: 75 Minutes

ISEE Upper Level Practice Test Answer Sheets

Remove (or photocopy) this answer sheet and use it to complete the practice test.

ISEE Upper Level Practice Test 2			
Quantitative Reasoning		**Mathematics Achievement**	

Quantitative Reasoning

1 Ⓐ Ⓑ Ⓒ Ⓓ   25 Ⓐ Ⓑ Ⓒ Ⓓ
2 Ⓐ Ⓑ Ⓒ Ⓓ   26 Ⓐ Ⓑ Ⓒ Ⓓ
3 Ⓐ Ⓑ Ⓒ Ⓓ   27 Ⓐ Ⓑ Ⓒ Ⓓ
4 Ⓐ Ⓑ Ⓒ Ⓓ   28 Ⓐ Ⓑ Ⓒ Ⓓ
5 Ⓐ Ⓑ Ⓒ Ⓓ   29 Ⓐ Ⓑ Ⓒ Ⓓ
6 Ⓐ Ⓑ Ⓒ Ⓓ   30 Ⓐ Ⓑ Ⓒ Ⓓ
7 Ⓐ Ⓑ Ⓒ Ⓓ   31 Ⓐ Ⓑ Ⓒ Ⓓ
8 Ⓐ Ⓑ Ⓒ Ⓓ   32 Ⓐ Ⓑ Ⓒ Ⓓ
9 Ⓐ Ⓑ Ⓒ Ⓓ   33 Ⓐ Ⓑ Ⓒ Ⓓ
10 Ⓐ Ⓑ Ⓒ Ⓓ   34 Ⓐ Ⓑ Ⓒ Ⓓ
11 Ⓐ Ⓑ Ⓒ Ⓓ   35 Ⓐ Ⓑ Ⓒ Ⓓ
12 Ⓐ Ⓑ Ⓒ Ⓓ   36 Ⓐ Ⓑ Ⓒ Ⓓ
13 Ⓐ Ⓑ Ⓒ Ⓓ   37 Ⓐ Ⓑ Ⓒ Ⓓ
14 Ⓐ Ⓑ Ⓒ Ⓓ
15 Ⓐ Ⓑ Ⓒ Ⓓ
16 Ⓐ Ⓑ Ⓒ Ⓓ
17 Ⓐ Ⓑ Ⓒ Ⓓ
18 Ⓐ Ⓑ Ⓒ Ⓓ
19 Ⓐ Ⓑ Ⓒ Ⓓ
20 Ⓐ Ⓑ Ⓒ Ⓓ
21 Ⓐ Ⓑ Ⓒ Ⓓ
22 Ⓐ Ⓑ Ⓒ Ⓓ
23 Ⓐ Ⓑ Ⓒ Ⓓ
24 Ⓐ Ⓑ Ⓒ Ⓓ

Mathematics Achievement

1 Ⓐ Ⓑ Ⓒ Ⓓ   25 Ⓐ Ⓑ Ⓒ Ⓓ
2 Ⓐ Ⓑ Ⓒ Ⓓ   26 Ⓐ Ⓑ Ⓒ Ⓓ
3 Ⓐ Ⓑ Ⓒ Ⓓ   27 Ⓐ Ⓑ Ⓒ Ⓓ
4 Ⓐ Ⓑ Ⓒ Ⓓ   28 Ⓐ Ⓑ Ⓒ Ⓓ
5 Ⓐ Ⓑ Ⓒ Ⓓ   29 Ⓐ Ⓑ Ⓒ Ⓓ
6 Ⓐ Ⓑ Ⓒ Ⓓ   30 Ⓐ Ⓑ Ⓒ Ⓓ
7 Ⓐ Ⓑ Ⓒ Ⓓ   31 Ⓐ Ⓑ Ⓒ Ⓓ
8 Ⓐ Ⓑ Ⓒ Ⓓ   32 Ⓐ Ⓑ Ⓒ Ⓓ
9 Ⓐ Ⓑ Ⓒ Ⓓ   33 Ⓐ Ⓑ Ⓒ Ⓓ
10 Ⓐ Ⓑ Ⓒ Ⓓ   34 Ⓐ Ⓑ Ⓒ Ⓓ
11 Ⓐ Ⓑ Ⓒ Ⓓ   35 Ⓐ Ⓑ Ⓒ Ⓓ
12 Ⓐ Ⓑ Ⓒ Ⓓ   36 Ⓐ Ⓑ Ⓒ Ⓓ
13 Ⓐ Ⓑ Ⓒ Ⓓ   37 Ⓐ Ⓑ Ⓒ Ⓓ
14 Ⓐ Ⓑ Ⓒ Ⓓ   38 Ⓐ Ⓑ Ⓒ Ⓓ
15 Ⓐ Ⓑ Ⓒ Ⓓ   39 Ⓐ Ⓑ Ⓒ Ⓓ
16 Ⓐ Ⓑ Ⓒ Ⓓ   40 Ⓐ Ⓑ Ⓒ Ⓓ
17 Ⓐ Ⓑ Ⓒ Ⓓ   41 Ⓐ Ⓑ Ⓒ Ⓓ
18 Ⓐ Ⓑ Ⓒ Ⓓ   42 Ⓐ Ⓑ Ⓒ Ⓓ
19 Ⓐ Ⓑ Ⓒ Ⓓ   43 Ⓐ Ⓑ Ⓒ Ⓓ
20 Ⓐ Ⓑ Ⓒ Ⓓ   44 Ⓐ Ⓑ Ⓒ Ⓓ
21 Ⓐ Ⓑ Ⓒ Ⓓ   45 Ⓐ Ⓑ Ⓒ Ⓓ
22 Ⓐ Ⓑ Ⓒ Ⓓ   46 Ⓐ Ⓑ Ⓒ Ⓓ
23 Ⓐ Ⓑ Ⓒ Ⓓ   47 Ⓐ Ⓑ Ⓒ Ⓓ
24 Ⓐ Ⓑ Ⓒ Ⓓ

ISEE Upper Level Practice Test 2

Part 1 (Quantitative Reasoning)

37 questions

Total time for this section: 35 Minutes

You may NOT use a calculator for this test.

1) If $2y + 6 < 30$, then y could be equal to?

A. 15

B. 14

C. 12

D. 8

2) Which of the following is NOT a factor of 90?

A. 9

B. 10

C. 16

D. 30

3) What is the area of a square whose diagonal is 6 meters?

A. $20\ m^2$

B. $18\ m^2$

C. $12\ m^2$

D. $10\ m^2$

4) If Emily left a $13.26 tip on a breakfast that cost $58.56, approximately what percentage was the tip?

A. 24%

B. 22%

C. 20%

D. 18%

5) There are 7 blue marbles, 9 red marbles, and 6 yellow marbles in a box. If Ava randomly selects a marble from the box, what is the probability of selecting a red or yellow marble?

A. $\frac{1}{7}$

B. $\frac{1}{9}$

C. $\frac{15}{22}$

D. $\frac{5}{7}$

6) James earns $8.50 per hour and worked 20 hours. Jacob earns $10.00 per hour. How many hours would Jacob need to work to equal James's earnings over 20 hours?

A. 14

B. 17

C. 20

D. 25

7) A phone company charges $5 for the first five minutes of a phone call and 50 cents per minute thereafter. If Sofia makes a phone call that lasts 30 minutes, what will be the total cost of the phone call?

A. 18.00

B. 18.50

C. 20.00

D. 20.50

8) Michelle and Alec can finish a job together in 50 minutes. If Michelle can do the job by herself in 2.5 hours, how many minutes does it take Alec to finish the job?

A. 100

B. 75

C. 50

D. 40

9) If 150% of a number is 75, then what is the 90% of that number?

A. 45

B. 50

C. 60

D. 70

10) In the figure, MN is 50 cm. How long is ON?

A. 35 cm

B. 30 cm

C. 25 cm

D. 20 cm

11) On a map, the length of the road from City A to City B is measured to be 18 inches. On this map, $\frac{1}{2}$ inch represents an actual distance of 14 miles. What is the actual distance, in miles, from City A to City B along this road?

A. 504 miles

B. 620 miles

C. 860 miles

D. 1,260 miles

A library has 700 books that include Mathematics, Physics, Chemistry, English and History.

Use following graph to answer questions 12.

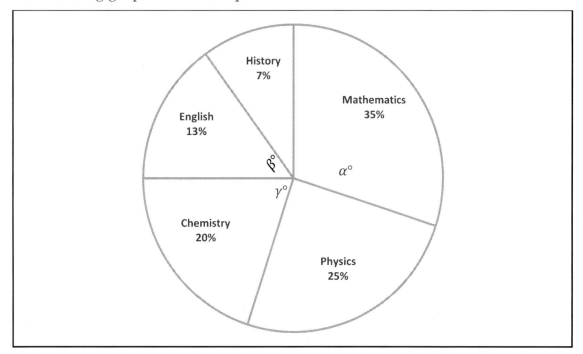

12) What is the product of the number of Mathematics and number of English books?

A. 10,870

B. 18,452

C. 22,295

D. 35,265

13) How many $\frac{1}{6}$ pound paperback books together weigh 60 pounds?

A. 100

B. 200

C. 300

D. 360

14) Emily and Daniel have taken the same number of photos on their school trip. Emily has taken 6 times as many as photos as Claire and Daniel has taken 15 more photos than Claire. How many photos has Claire taken?

A. 2

B. 3

C. 9

D. 11

15) The first four terms in a sequence are shown below. What is the sixth term in the sequence?

$$\{3, 6, 11, 18, \dots\}$$

A. 38

B. 40

C. 45

D. 50

16) What is the equation of the line that passes through $(3, -3)$ and has a slope of 2?

A. $y = 2x - 9$

B. $y = 3x - 3$

C. $y = 2x + 3$

D. $y = 3x + 9$

17) Find the solution (x, y) to the following system of equations?

$$-4x - y = 8$$

$$8x + 6y = 20$$

A. $(5, 14)$

B. $(8, 6)$

C. $(17, 11)$

D. $(-\frac{17}{4}, 9)$

18) Sophia purchased a sofa for $530.20. The sofa is regularly priced at $631. What was the percent discount Sophia received on the sofa?

A. 12%

B. 16%

C. 21%

D. 26%

19) Three second of 20 is equal to $\frac{5}{2}$ of what number?

A. 12

B. 20

C. 40

D. 60

20) A supermarket's sales increased by 11 percent in the month of April and decreased by 11 percent in the month of May. What is the percent change in the sales of the supermarket over the two-month period?

A. 2% decrease

B. No change

C. 2% increase

D. 2.2% increase

21) The distance between cities A and B is approximately 2,700 miles. If Alice drives an average of 74 miles per hour, how many hours will it take Alice to drive from city A to city B?

A. *Approximately* 41 *hours*

B. *Approximately* 36 *hours*

C. *Approximately* 28 *hours*

D. *Approximately* 21 *hours*

22)

Quantitative Comparisons

Direction: Questions 22 to 37 are Quantitative Comparisons Questions. Using the information provided in each question, compare the quantity in column A to the quantity in Column B. Choose on your answer sheet grid

A. if the quantity in Column A is greater

B. if the quantity in Column B is greater

C. if the two quantities are equal

D. if the relationship cannot be determined from the information given

23) $x^2 = 8$

Column A	Column B
x	2

24) For all numbers x and y, let the function $x \diamondsuit y$ be defined by $x \diamondsuit y = x^2 - 2xy + y^2$

Column A	Column B
$4 \diamondsuit 5$	$5 \diamondsuit 4$

25)

Column A	Column B
The average of $16, 22, 24, 36, 40$	The average of $28, 33, 38, 42$

26)

Column A	Column B
$\dfrac{1}{x+1}$	$\dfrac{2}{x+2}$

27) $\dfrac{x}{3} = y^2$

Column A	Column B
x	y

28) $x = 1$

Column A	Column B
$2x^3 - 3x - 2$	$3x^2 - 2x - 3$

29)

Column A	Column B
$8 + 14(7 - 3)$	$14 + 8(7 - 3)$

30) $\dfrac{x}{36} = \dfrac{3}{4}$

Column A	Column B
$\dfrac{9}{x}$	$\dfrac{1}{9}$

31) Working at constant rates, machine D makes b rolls of steel in 38 minutes and machine E makes b rolls of steel in one hour ($b > 0$)

Column A	Column B
The number of rolls of steel made by machine D in 3 hours and 10 minutes.	The number of rolls of steel made by machine E in 5 hours.

32) $-1 < y < 4$

Column A	Column B
$\dfrac{y}{2}$	$\dfrac{2}{y}$

33) $\dfrac{a}{b} = \dfrac{c}{d}$

Column A	Column B
$a + b$	$c + d$

34) The ratio of boys to girls in a class is 5 to 7.

Column A	Column B
Ratio of boys to the entire class	$\dfrac{1}{3}$

35) There are only 4 blue marbles and 5 green marbles in a jar. Two marbles are pulled out in succession without replacing them in the jar.

Column A	Column B
The probability that both marbles are blue.	The probability that the first marbles is green, but the second is blue.

36) A magazine printer consecutively numbered the pages of a magazine, starting with 1 on the first page, 10 on the tenth page, etc. In numbering the gages, the printer printed a total of 195 digits.

Column A	Column B
The number of pages in the magazine	100

37)

Column A	Column B
The largest number that can be written by rearranging the digits in 381	The largest number that can be written by rearranging the digits in 279

STOP: This is the End of Section 1 of test 2.

ISEE Upper Level

Practice Test 2

Part 2 (Mathematics Achievement)

47 questions

Total time for this section: 40 Minutes

You may NOT use a calculator for this test.

1) How is this number written in scientific notation?

0.00003379

A. 3.379×10^{-5}

B. 33.79×10^{6}

C. 0.3379×10^{-4}

D. 3379×10^{-8}

2) $|10 - (12 \div |1 - 5|)| = ?$

A. 7

B. -7

C. 5

D. -5

3) $(x + 4)(x + 5) =$

A. $x^2 + 9x + 20$

B. $2x + 12x + 12$

C. $x^2 + 25x + 10$

D. $x^2 + 12x + 35$

4) Find all values of x for which $6x^2 + 16x + 8 = 0$

A. $-\frac{3}{2}, -\frac{1}{2}$

B. $-\frac{2}{3}, -2$

C. $-2, -\frac{1}{4}$

D. $-\frac{2}{3}, \frac{1}{2}$

5) Which of the following graphs represents the compound inequality $-2 \leq$

 $2x - 4 < 8$?

A.

B.

C.

D.

6) $1 - 9 \div (4^2 \div 2) = $ ___

A. 6

B. $\frac{3}{4}$

C. $-\frac{1}{8}$

D. -2

7) A girl 200 *cm* tall, stands 460 *cm* from a lamp post at night. Her shadow from the light is 80 *cm* long. How high is the lamp post?

A. 440

B. 500

C. 900

D. 1350

8) Which graph corresponds to the following inequality?

$$-6y \leq 16x - 12$$

☐A.

☐B.

☐C.

☐D.

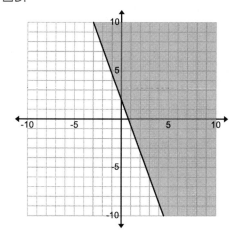

9) The ratio of boys to girls in a school is $3:5$. If there are 600 students in a school, how many boys are in the school?

A. 200

B. 225

C. 300

D. 340

10) $90 \div \frac{1}{9} = ?$

A. 9.125

B. 10

C. 81

D. 810

11) The rectangle on the coordinate grid is translated 5 units down and 4 units to the left.

Which of the following describes this transformation?

A. $(x, y) \Rightarrow (x - 4, y + 5)$

B. $(x, y) \Rightarrow (x - 4, y - 5)$

C. $(x, y) \Rightarrow (x + 4, y + 5)$

D. $(x, y) \Rightarrow (x + 4, y - 5)$

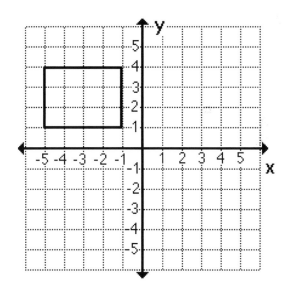

12) Find the area of a rectangle with a length of 148 feet and a width of 90 feet.

A. 13,320 $sq.ft$

B. 13,454 $sq.ft$

C. 13,404 $sq.ft$

D. 13,204 $sq.ft$

13) Which value of x makes the following inequality true?

$$\frac{4}{23} \leq x < 25\%$$

A. 0.12

B. $\frac{5}{36}$

C. $\sqrt{0.044}$

D. 0.104

14) Which of the following could be the product of two consecutive prime numbers?

A. 2

B. 10

C. 14

D. 15

15) The perimeter of the trapezoid below is 38 cm. What is its area?

A. 576 cm^2

B. 78 cm^2

C. 48 cm^2

D. 24cm^2

16) Emily lives $4\frac{1}{5}$ miles from where she works. When traveling to work, she walks to a bus stop $\frac{1}{2}$ of the way to catch a bus. How many miles away from her house is the bus stop?

A. $2\frac{1}{10}$ $miles$

B. $4\frac{3}{10}$ $miles$

C. $2\frac{3}{10}$ $miles$

D. $1\frac{3}{10}miles$

17) If a vehicle is driven 40 miles on Monday, 45 miles on Tuesday, and 50 miles on Wednesday, what is the average number of miles driven each day?

A. 40 *miles*

B. 45 *miles*

C. 50 *miles*

D. 53 *miles*

18) Use the diagram below to answer the question.

Given the lengths of the base and diagonal of the rectangle below, what is the length of height h, in terms of s?

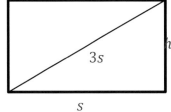

A. $s\sqrt{2}$

B. $2s\sqrt{2}$

C. $3s$

D. $3s^2$

Use the chart below to answer the question.

Color	Number
White	40
Black	30
Beige	40

19) There are also purple marbles in the bag. Which of the following can NOT be the probability of randomly selecting a purple marble from the bag?

A. $\frac{1}{11}$

B. $\frac{1}{6}$

C. $\frac{2}{5}$

D. $\frac{1}{23}$

20) With an 23% discount, Ella was able to save $21.87 on a dress. What was the original price of the dress?

A. $89.92

B. $91.82

C. $95.09

D. $97.92

21) $\frac{8}{35}$ is equals to:

A. 0.28

B. 2.28

C. 0.028

D. 0.228

22) If 30% of A is 1,200, what is 12% of A?

A. 280

B. 480

C. 1,200

D. 1600

23) Simplify $\dfrac{\frac{1}{3} - \frac{x-5}{9}}{\frac{x^3}{3} - \frac{7}{3}}$

A. $\dfrac{7+x}{3x^3+21}$

B. $\dfrac{-7-x}{x^3-21}$

C. $\dfrac{7+x}{x^3-21}$

D. $\dfrac{7-x}{3x^3-21}$

24) If $(6.2 + 8.3 + 2.4) \times x = x$, then what is the value of x?

A. 0

B. $\frac{3}{10}$

C. −6

D. −12

25) Two dice are thrown simultaneously, what is the probability of getting a sum of 5 or 8?

A. $\frac{1}{3}$

B. $\frac{1}{4}$

C. $\frac{1}{16}$

D. $\frac{11}{36}$

26) If 7 garbage trucks can collect the trash of 38 homes in a day. How many trucks are needed to collect in 190 houses?

A. 20

B. 30

C. 35

D. 40

27) $78.56 \div 0.05 = ?$

A. 15.712

B. 1,571.2

C. 157.12

D. 1.5712

28) In the following figure, AB is the diameter of the circle. What is the circumference of the circle?

A. 4π

B. 6π

C. 8π

D. 10π

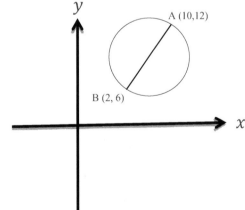

29) What is the value of x in the following equation?

$$2x^2 + 6 = 26$$

A. ± 4

B. $\pm \sqrt{9}$

C. $\pm \sqrt{10}$

D. ± 3

30) A circle has a diameter of 20 inches. What is its approximate area?

A. $314 \ inch^2$

B. $114 \ inch^2$

C. $74.00 \ inch^2$

D. $12.56 \ inch^2$

31) $6 \ days \ 20 \ hours \ 36 \ minutes - 4 \ days \ 12 \ hours \ 24 \ minutes \ = \ ?$

A. $2 \ days \ 8 \ hours \ 12 \ minutes$

B. $1 \ days \ 8 \ hours \ 12 \ minutes$

C. $2 \ days \ 7 \ hours \ 14 \ minutes$

D. $1 \ days \ 7 \ hours \ 14 \ minutes$

32) The base of a right triangle is 4 feet, and the interior angles are $45 - 45 - 90$. What is its area?

A. $2 \ square \ feet$

B. $4 \ square \ feet$

C. $8 \ square \ feet$

D. $10 \ square \ feet$

Use the following table to answer question below.

DANIEL'S BIRD-WATCHING PROJECT	
DAY	NUMBER OF RAPTORS SEEN
Monday	?
Tuesday	10
Wednesday	15
Thursday	13
Friday	6
MEAN	11

33) The above table shows the data Daniel collects while watching birds for one week. How many raptors did Daniel see on Monday?

A. 10

B. 11

C. 12

D. 13

34) A floppy disk shows 837,036 bytes free and 639,352 bytes used. If you delete a file of size 542,159 bytes and create a new file of size 499,986 bytes, how many free bytes will the floppy disk have?

A. 567,179 bytes

B. 671,525 bytes

C. 879,209 bytes

D. 899,209 bytes

35) Increased by 40%, the number 70 becomes:

A. 40

B. 98

C. 126

D. 130

36) If $12 + x^{\frac{1}{2}} = 24$, then what is the value of $5 \times x$?

A. 15

B. 60

C. 240

D. 720

37) Which equation represents the statement "twice the difference between 5 times H and 2 gives 35".

A. $\frac{5H + 2}{2} = 35$

B. $5(2H + 2) = 35$

C. $2(5H - 2) = 35$

D. $2 \frac{5H}{2} = 35$

38) A circle is inscribed in a square, as shown below.

The area of the circle is $25\pi \ cm^2$ What is the area of the square?

A. $10 \ cm^2$

B. $26 \ cm^2$

C. $48 \ cm^2$

D. $100 \ cm^2$

39) Triangle ABC is graphed on a coordinate grid with vertices at $A \ (-2, -3)$, $B \ (-4, 1)$ and $C \ (9, 7)$. Triangle ABC is reflected over x axes to create triangle $A'B'C'$.

Which order pair represents the coordinate of C'?

A. $(9, 7)$

B. $(-9, -7)$

C. $(9, -7)$

D. $(7, -9)$

40) Which set of ordered pairs represents y as a function of x?

A. $\{(5, -2), (5, 7), (9, -8), (4, -7)\}$

B. $\{(2, 2), (3, -9), (5, 8), (2, 7)\}$

C. $\{(9, 12), (8, 7), (6, 11), (8, 18)\}$

D. $\{(6, 1), (3, 1), (0, 5), (6, 1)\}$

41) The width of a box is one third of its length. The height of the box is one half of its width. If the length of the box is 24 cm, what is the volume of the box?

A. $80 cm^3$

B. $165\ cm^3$

C. $243\ cm^3$

D. $768 cm^3$

42) How many 4×4 squares can fit inside a rectangle with a height of 40 and width of 12?

A. 60

B. 50

C. 40

D. 30

43) David makes a weekly salary of $230 plus 9% commission on his sales. What will his income be for a week in which he makes sales totaling $1,200?

A. $338

B. $318

C. $308

D. $298

44) $5x^3y^2 + 4x^5y^3 - (6x^3y^2 - 4xy^5) =$ ___

A. $4x^5y^3$

B. $4x^5y^3 - x^3y^2 + 4xy^5$

C. $C.x^3y^2$

D. $4x^5y^3 - x^3y^2$

45) The radius of circle *A* is five times the radius of circle *B*. If the circumference of circle *A* is 20π, what is the area of circle *B*?

A. 3π

B. 4π

C. 6π

D. 12π

46) A square measures 8 inches on one side. By how much will the area be decreased if its length is increased by 5 inches and its width decreased by 4 inches.

A. 1 *sq decreased*

B. 3 *sq decreased*

C. 8 *sq decreased*

D. 12 *sq decreased*

47) If a box contains red and blue balls in ratio of 3 : 2 red to blue, how many red balls are there if 80 blue balls are in the box?

A. 60

B. 80

C. 100

D. 120

STOP: This is the End of Section 2 of test 2.

ISEE Upper Level Practice Tests Answer Keys

Now, it's time to review your results to see where you went wrong and what areas you need to improve!

ISEE Upper Level Math Practice Test 1 Answer Key										
Quantitative Reasoning					Mathematics Achievement					
1	B	17	B	33	C	1	B	17	B	33	D
2	B	18	B	34	A	2	B	18	B	34	A
3	C	19	B	35	A	3	B	19	B	35	B
4	D	20	B	36	A	4	D	20	C	36	C
5	D	21	B	37	D	5	D	21	C	37	D
6	D	22	A			6	A	22	D	38	D
7	A	23	B			7	B	23	B	39	A
8	C	24	D			8	B	24	A	40	B
9	C	25	A			9	D	25	A	41	C
10	D	26	D			10	D	26	B	42	C
11	C	27	D			11	C	27	C	43	C
12	C	28	C			12	C	28	B	44	B
13	D	29	A			13	C	29	C	45	A
14	D	30	A			14	C	30	C	46	B
15	B	31	B			15	B	31	D	47	B
16	C	32	B			16	A	32	C		

ISEE Upper Level Math Practice Test 2 Answer Key

Quantitative Reasoning

1	D	17	D	33	A
2	C	18	B	34	B
3	B	19	A	35	A
4	B	20	A	36	B
5	C	21	B	37	A
6	B	22	D		
7	C	23	C		
8	B	24	B		
9	A	25	D		
10	B	26	D		
11	A	27	B		
12	C	28	A		
13	D	29	A		
14	B	30	C		
15	A	31	D		
16	A	32	D		

Mathematics Achievement

1	A	17	B	33	B
2	A	18	B	34	C
3	A	19	C	35	B
4	B	20	C	36	D
5	D	21	D	37	C
6	C	22	B	38	D
7	D	23	B	39	C
8	D	24	A	40	D
9	B	25	B	41	D
10	D	26	C	42	D
11	B	27	B	43	A
12	A	28	D	44	B
13	C	29	C	45	B
14	D	30	A	46	D
15	B	31	A	47	D
16	A	32	C		

Score Your Test

ISEE scores are broken down by four sections: Verbal Reasoning, Reading Comprehension, Quantitative Reasoning, and Mathematics Achievement. A sum of the ALL sections is also reported. The Essay section is scored separately.

For the Upper Level ISEE, the score range is 760 to 940, the lowest possible score a student can earn is 760 and the highest score is 940 for each section. A student receives 1 point for every correct answer. There is no penalty for wrong or skipped questions.

The total scaled score for an Upper Level ISEE test is the sum of the scores for all sections. A student will also receive a percentile score of between 1-99% that compares that student's test scores with those of other test takers of same grade and gender from the past 3 years. When a student receives her/his score, the percentile score is also be broken down into a stanine and the stanines are ranging from 1–9. Most schools accept students with scores of 5–9. The ideal candidate has scores of 6 or higher.

Percentile Rank	Stanine
1 – 3	1
4 – 10	2
11- 22	3
23 - 39	4
40 – 59	5
60 – 76	6
77- 88	7
89 – 95	8
96 - 99	9

The following charts provide an estimate of students ISEE percentile rankings for the practice tests, compared against other students taking these tests. Keep in mind that these percentiles are estimates only, and your actual ISEE percentile will depend on the specific group of students taking the exam in your year.

ISEE Upper Level Quantitative Reasoning Percentiles			
Grade Applying to	25th Percentile	50th Percentile	75th Percentile
9th	850	880	895
10th	855	885	900
11th	860	890	905
12th	864	892	908

Use the next table to convert ISEE Upper level raw score to scaled score for application to 9th - 12th grade.

ISEE Upper Level Scaled Scores								
Raw Score	Quantitative Reasoning Report Range		Mathematics Achievement Report Range		Raw Score	Quantitative Reasoning Report Range		Mathematics Achievement Report Range	
0	760	760	760	760	26	900	885	885	865
1	770	765	770	765	27	905	890	885	865
2	780	770	780	770	28	910	895	890	870
3	790	775	790	775	29	910	900	890	870
4	800	780	800	780	30	915	905	895	875
5	810	785	810	785	31	920	910	895	875
6	820	790	820	790	32	925	915	900	880
7	825	795	825	795	33	930	920	900	880
8	830	800	830	800	34	930	925	905	885
9	835	805	835	805	35	935	930	905	885
10	840	810	840	810	36	935	935	910	890
11	845	815	845	815	37	940	940	910	890
12	850	820	850	820	38			915	895
13	855	825	855	825	39			920	900
14	860	830	855	830	40			925	905
15	865	835	860	835	41			925	910
16	870	840	860	840	42			930	915
17	875	845	865	840	43			930	920
18	880	845	865	845	44			935	925
19	880	850	870	845	45			935	930
20	885	855	870	850	46			940	935
21	885	860	875	850	47			940	940
22	890	865	875	855					
23	890	870	875	855					
24	895	875	880	860					
25	895	880	880	860					

ISEE Upper Level Practice Tests Answers and Explanations

ISEE Upper Level Practice Test 1
Quantitative Reasoning

1) Choice B is correct

Find the value of each choice:

$2 \times 2 \times 5 \times 7 = 140, 2 \times 2 \times 2 \times 2 \times 5 \times 7 = 560, 2 \times 7 = 14, 2 \times 2 \times 2 \times 5 \times 7 = 280$

2) Choice B is correct

Recall that the formula for the average is: $Average = \frac{sum\ of\ data}{number\ of\ data}$

First, compute the total weight of all balls in the basket: $25 = \frac{total\ weight}{20\ balls}$

$25g \times 20 = total\ weight = 500\ g$

Next, find the total weight of the 5 largest marbles: $40g = \frac{total\ weight}{5\ marbles}$

$40\ g \times 5 = total\ weight = 200\ g$

The total weight of the heaviest balls is $200\ g$. Then, the total weight of the remaining 15 balls is $300\ g$. $500\ g - 200\ g = 300\ g$.

The average weight of the remaining balls: $Average = \frac{300\ g}{15\ marbles} = 20\ g\ per\ ball$

3) Choice C is correct

$(5x + 8) - (5x - 3) = 5x - 5x + 8 + 3 = 11$

4) Choice D is correct

Write a proportion and solve. $\frac{5in}{100feet} = \frac{18in}{x} \rightarrow x = \frac{100 \times 18}{5} = 360$ feet

5) Choice D is correct

Let x be all expenses, then $\frac{22}{100}x = \$660 \rightarrow x = \frac{100 \times \$660}{22} = \$3,000$

He spent for his rent: $\frac{27}{100} \times \$3,000 = \$810$

6) Choice D is correct

There is not enough information to determine the answer of the question. An average speed represents a distance divided by time and it does not provide information about the speed at specific time. Alice could drove exactly 55 miles per hour from start to finish, or she could drive 65 miles per hour for half of distance and 45 miles per hour for the other half.

7) Choice A is correct

Area of the circle is less than $64\,\pi$. Use the formula of areas of circles.

$Area = \pi r^2 \Rightarrow 64\,\pi > \pi r^2 \Rightarrow 64 > r^2 \Rightarrow r < 8$

Radius of the circle is less than 8. Let's put 8 for the radius. Now, use the circumference formula: $Circumference = 2\pi r = 2\pi\,(8) = 16\,\pi$. Since the radius of the circle is less than 8. Then, the circumference of the circle must be less than $16\,\pi$. Only choice A is less than $16\,\pi$.

8) Choice C is correct

The percentage discount is the reduction in price divided by the original price. The difference between original price and sale price is: $\$12.65 - \$7.35 = \$5.3$

The percentage discount is this difference divided by the original price: $\$5.3 \div \$12.65 \cong 0.42$

Convert the decimal to a percentage by multiplying by 100%: $0.42 \times 100\% = 42\%$

9) Choice C is correct

The smallest possible value of $f(x)$ will occur when $x = 0$. Since x^2 is always positive, any positive or negative value of x will make the value of $f(x)$ greater than 5. Substitute 0 for x and evaluate the expression: $f(0) = (0)^2 + 5 = 5$

10) Choice D is correct

There are 2 sets of values, one set from 1 to n, and the other set from $n + 1$ to $2n$. Since the second set begins immediately after the first set, the two sets can be combined. The sum of the positive integers from 1 to $2n$ inclusive is equal to the sum of the positive integers from 1 to n plus the sum of the positive integers from $n + 1$ to $2n$: $2,250 + 4,356 = 6,606$

11) Choice C is correct

Let's review the choices provided:

A. Number of books sold in April is: 380

Number of books sold in July is: $760 \rightarrow \dfrac{380}{760} = \dfrac{38}{76} = \dfrac{1}{2}$

B. number of books sold in July is: 760

Half the number of books sold in May is: $\dfrac{1140}{2} = 570 \rightarrow 760 > 570$

C. number of books sold in June is: 190

Half the number of books sold in April is: $\dfrac{380}{2} = 190 \rightarrow 190 = 190$

D. $380 + 190 = 570 < 760$

Only choice C is correct.

12) Choice C is correct

The median of a set of data is the value located in the middle of the data set. Combine the 2 sets provided, and organize them in ascending order: $\{1, 3, 4, 6, 8, 10, 12, 14, 15, 17\}$

Since there are an even number of items in the resulting list, the median is the average of the two middle numbers. $Median = (8 + 10) \div 2 = 9$

13) Choice D is correct

Let x be the number of current stamps in the collection. Then: $\frac{6}{5}x - x = 100 \rightarrow$
$\frac{1}{5}x = 100 \rightarrow x = 500$, 50% more of 500 is: $500 + 0.50 \times 500 = 500 + 250 = 750$

14) Choice D is correct

If 17 balls are removed from the bag at random, there will be one ball in the bag. The probability of choosing a brown ball is 1 out of 18. Therefore, the probability of not choosing a brown ball is 17 out of 18 and the probability of having not a brown ball after removing 17 balls is the same.

15) Choice B is correct

$(x^2 - y^2) = (x - y)(x + y)$, Then: $x^2 - y^2 = 5 \times 8 = 40$

16) Choice C is correct

The ratio of boy to girls is $4 : 7$. Therefore, there are 4 boys out of 11 students. To find the answer, first divide the total number of students by 11, then multiply the result by 4.

$44 \div 11 = 4 \Rightarrow 4 \times 4 = 16$, There are 16 boys and $28 (44 - 16)$ girls. So, $12 (28 - 16)$ more boys should be enrolled to make the ratio $1 : 1$.

17) Choice B is correct

The formula for the area of a rectangle is: $Area = Width \times Length$

It is given that $L = 4 W$ and that $A = 196$ square inches. Substitute the given values into our equation and solve for W: $196 = w \times 4w$, $196 = 4w^2$, $w^2 = 49$, $w = 7$. It is given that $L = 4W$, therefore, $L = 4 \times 7 = 28$, The perimeter of a rectangle is: $2L + 2W$

Perimeter $= 2 \times 28 + 2 \times 7$, Perimeter $= 70$ inches

18) Choice B is correct

The sum of 8 numbers is greater than 160 and less than 240. Then, the average of the 8 numbers must be greater than 20 and less than 30. $\frac{160}{8} < x < \frac{240}{8}$

$20 < x < 30$, The only choice that is between 20 and 30 is 25.

19) Choice B is correct

In order to solve for the variable b, first take square roots on both sides: $\sqrt{a} = \frac{cz}{b}$, then multiply both sides by b: $b\sqrt{a} = cz$, Now, divide both sides by $\sqrt{a}$: $b = \frac{cz}{\sqrt{a}}$

20) Choice B is correct

If two triangles are similar, then the ratios of corresponding sides are equal.

$\frac{AC}{AE} = \frac{BC}{DE} = \frac{18}{9} = 2, \frac{AC}{AE} = 2$

This ratio can be used to find the length of AC: $AC = 2 \times AE$, $AC = 2 \times 9$, $AC = 18$

The length of AE is given as 9 and we now know the length of AC is 18, therefore:

$EC = AC - AE$, $EC = 18 - 9$, $EC = 9$

21) Choice B is correct

Let x be number of gallons the tank can hold when it is full. Then: $\frac{2}{5}x = 25 \rightarrow x = \frac{5}{2} \times 25 = 62.5$

22) Choice A is correct

The average is the sum of all terms divided by the number of terms.

$15 + 25 + 27 = 67$, $67 \div 3 = 22.33$. This is greater than 20.

23) Choice B is correct

Since both columns have 675 as a factor, we can ignore that number.

$11 \times 24 = 264$, $18 \times 17 = 306$. Column B is greater

24) Choice D is correct

Since x is an integer and can be positive and negative, then the relationship cannot be determined from the information given. Let's choose some values for x.

$x = 1$, then the value in column A is greater. $1 > \frac{1}{-2}$

Let's choose a negative value for x. $x = -1$, then the value in column B is greater.

$-1 < \frac{-1}{-2} \rightarrow -1 < \frac{1}{2}$

25)Choice A is correct

First, find the values of x in both columns.

Column A: $6|2x - 4| = 6 \rightarrow |2x - 4| = 1$

$2x - 4$ can be 1 or -1.

$2x - 4 = 1 \rightarrow 2x = 5 \rightarrow x = \dfrac{5}{2}$

$2x - 4 = -1 \rightarrow 2x = 3 \rightarrow x = \dfrac{3}{2}$

Column B: $6|2x + 4| = 6 \rightarrow |2x + 4| = 1$

$2x + 4$ can be 1 or -1.

$2x + 4 = 1 \rightarrow 2x = -3 \rightarrow x = -\dfrac{3}{2}$

$2x + 4 = -1 \rightarrow 2x = -5 \rightarrow x = -\dfrac{5}{2}$

The greatest value of x in column A is $\dfrac{5}{2}$ and the greatest value of x in column B is $-\dfrac{3}{2}$.

26)Choice D is correct

Simplify both columns.

Column A: $(x)^3(x)^4 = x^7$

Column B: $(x^3)^4 = x^{12}$

Column A evaluates to x^7 and Column B evaluates to x^{12}. In the case where $x = 0$, the two columns will be equal, but if $x = 2$, the two columns will not be equal. Consequently, the relationship cannot be determined.

27)Choice D is correct

The probability that an event will occur + the probability that that event will NOT occur must equal 1. Since we don't have any numerical information about the probability, it is possible that the probability that event x occurs is 25%, 50% or any other percent. The probability that event x will not occur will always be 100% minus the probability that event x does occur. Because both columns can exhibit a range of values, the relationship cannot be determined.

28)Choice C is correct

Column A: $2^2 = 4$, Column B: $\sqrt[3]{64} = 4$ (recall that $4^3 = 16$)

29) Choice A is correct

A number raised to the exponent $\frac{1}{2}$ is the same thing as evaluating the square root of the number. Therefore: $(59)^{\frac{1}{2}} = \sqrt{59}$, Since $\sqrt{64}$ is greater than $\sqrt{59}$, column A ($\sqrt{64} = 8$) is greater than $\sqrt{59}$.

30) Choice A is correct

Let x be the original price of the sport jacket. The selling price of a sport jacket including 25% discount is $51. Then: $x - 0.25x = 51 \rightarrow 0.75x = 51 \rightarrow x = \frac{51}{0.75} = 68$

The original price of the jacket is $68 which is greater than column B ($67).

31) Choice B is correct

The value of x has to be less than 50, which is less than 60. Column B is greater.

Recall that when the positive powers of numbers between 0 and 1 increases, the value of the number decrease. For example: $(0.5)^2 > (0.5)^3 \rightarrow 0.25 > 0.125$. So, $(0.69)^{33} > (0.69)^{34}$

32) Choice B is correct

Because of the word "and" the events described in each column must be calculated separately and then multiplied: For column A: Probability of rolling a 6: $\frac{1}{6}$

Probability of getting heads: $\frac{1}{2}, \frac{1}{6} \times \frac{1}{2} = \frac{1}{12}$

For column B: Probability of an even number: $\frac{3}{6} = \frac{1}{2}$

Probability of getting a spade: $\frac{13}{52} = \frac{1}{4}, \frac{1}{2} \times \frac{1}{4} = \frac{1}{8}$

Since $\frac{1}{8}$ is a larger number than $\frac{1}{12}$, Colum B is greater

33) Choice C is correct

To raise a quantity to a negative power, invert the numerator and denominator, and then raise the base to the indicated power. Therefore: $(\frac{5}{1})^{-2} = (\frac{1}{5})^2$, The Columns are the same value.

34) Choice A is correct

First, simplify the inequality: $x + 2 > 5x \rightarrow 2 > 4x \rightarrow \frac{2}{4} > x \rightarrow \frac{1}{2} > x$

Since x is less than $\frac{1}{2}$, and x can be 0 (greater than -1) or -2 (less than -1), the relationship cannot be determined.

35) Choice A is correct

Sum of one quarter, two nickels, and three pennies is: $\$0.25 + 2\ (\$0.05) + \$0.03 = \$0.38$

36) Choice A is correct

Let's consider the properties of odd and even integers:

$Odd\ +/-\ Odd\ = Even$

$Even\ +/-\ Even\ = Even$

$Odd\ +/-\ Even = Odd$

$Odd\ \times\ Odd\ = \ Odd$

$Even\ \times\ Even\ = \ Even$

$Odd\ \times\ Even\ = \ Even$

Now let's review the columns. For column A: $(x\ +\ y)^2 - y$

$(odd\ +\ even)^2 -\ even$

$(odd)^2 -\ even$

$(odd)(odd) - even$

$odd - even$

odd

For Column B:

$(y)(x\ -\ y)$

$(even)(odd - even)$

$(even)(odd)$

$even$

Since an odd number is considered greater according to the problem statement, the answer is A.

37) Choice D is correct

Factor the expression if possible. Begin by moving all terms to one side before factoring:

$x^2 - 5x - 8 = 6$

$x^2 - 5x - 14 = 0$

To factor this quadratic, find two numbers that multiply to -14 and sum to -5:

$(x - 7)(x + 2) = 0$

Set each expression in parentheses equal to 0 and solve: $x - 7 = 0$, $x = 7$

$x + 2 = 0$, $x = -2$

Quadratic equations can have TWO possible solutions. Since one of these is greater than 0 and one of them is less than 0, we cannot determine the relationship between the columns.

ISEE Upper Level Practice Test 1
Mathematics Achievement

1) Choice B is correct

Subtract $\frac{1}{6b}$ and $\frac{1}{b^2}$ from both sides of the equation. Then:

$$\frac{1}{6b^2} + \frac{1}{6b} = \frac{1}{b^2} \rightarrow \frac{1}{6b^2} - \frac{1}{b^2} = -\frac{1}{6b}$$

Multiply both numerator and denominator of the fraction $\frac{1}{b^2}$ by 6. Then:

$$\frac{1}{6b^2} - \frac{6}{6b^2} = -\frac{1}{6b}$$

Simplify the first side of the equation: $-\frac{5}{6b^2} = -\frac{1}{6b}$

Use cross multiplication method: $30b = 6b^2 \rightarrow 30 = 6b \rightarrow b = 5$

2) Choice B is correct

First, multiply both sides of inequality by 7. Then: $\frac{|3+x|}{7} \leq 5 \rightarrow |3 + x| \leq 35$

$$-35 \leq 3 + x \leq 35 \rightarrow -35 - 3 \leq x \leq 35 - 3 \rightarrow -38 \leq x \leq 32$$

3) Choice B is correct

Plug in the value of $x = 30$ into both equations. Then: $C(x) = x^2 + 2x = (30)^2 + 2(30) = 900 + 60 = 960$, $R(x) = 40x = 40 \times 30 = 1{,}200$, $1{,}200 - 960 = 240$. So, the profit is $240.

4) Choice D is correct

From choices provided, only choice D is correct. $E = 4 + A, A = S - 3$

5) Choice D is correct

Let x be the integer. Then: $2x - 5 = 83$, Add 5 both sides: $2x = 88$, Divide both sides by 2: $x = 44$

6) Choice A is correct.

Plug in each pair of numbers in the equation. The answer should be 14.

A. $(2, 1)$: $4(2) + 6(1) = 14$ Yes!

B. $(-1, 2)$: $4(-1) + 6(2) = 8$ No!

C. $(-2, 2)$: $4(-2) + 6(2) = 4$ No!

D. $(2, 2)$: $4(2) + 6(2) = 20$ No!

7) Choice B is correct

The sum of supplement angles is 180°. Let x be that angle. Therefore, $x + 5x = 180°$

$6x = 180°$, divide both sides by 6: $x = 30°$

8) Choice B is correct

$x\% \ 24 = 1.2, \dfrac{x}{100} \ 24 = 1.2 \rightarrow x = \dfrac{1.2 \times 100}{24} = 5$

9) Choice D is correct

Use Pythagorean Theorem: $a^2 + b^2 = c^2$, $6^2 + 8^2 = c^2 \Rightarrow 100 = c^2 \Rightarrow c = 10 \ cm$

10) Choice D is correct

Simplify. $6x^2y^3(2x^2y)^3 = 6x^2y^3(8x^6y^3) = 48x^8y^6$

11) Choice C is correct

$23 \ hours = 82,800 \ seconds, 1520 \ minutes = 91,200 \ seconds, 2 \ days = 48 \ hours = 172,800 \ seconds$

12) Choice C is correct

Let's review the choices provided:

A. $(5 \times 10^3) + (2 \times 10^2) + (3 \times 10) = 5,000 + 200 + 30 = 5,230$

B. $(5 \times 10^2) + (2 \times 10^1) - 5 = 500 + 20 - 5 = 515$

C. $(5 \times 10^2) + (2 \times 10^1) + 3 = 500 + 20 + 3 = 523$

D. $(5 \times 10^1) + (2 \times 10^2) + 3 = 50 + 200 + 3 = 253$

Only choice C equals to 523.

13) Choice C is correct

$\dfrac{4}{400} = \dfrac{x}{960}, x = \dfrac{4 \times 960}{400} = \$ \ 9.6$

14) Choice C is correct

Area of a circle equals: $A = \pi r^2$

The new diameter is 30% larger than the original then the new radius is also 30% larger than the original. 30% larger than r is $1.3r$. Then, the area of larger circle is:

$A = \pi r^2 = \pi(1.3r)^2 = \pi(1.69r^2) = 1.69\pi r^2$. $1.69\pi r^2$ is 69% bigger than πr^2.

15) Choice B is correct

$C = 2\pi r.\ C = 2\pi \times 4 = 8\pi,\ \pi = 3.14 \rightarrow C = 8\pi = 25.12$ inches

16) Choice A is correct

First draw an isosceles triangle. Remember that two sides of the triangle are equal.

Let put a for the legs. Then: Use Pythagorean theorem to find the value of a:

Isosceles right triangle

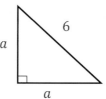

$a^2 + b^2 = c^2 \rightarrow a^2 + a^2 = 6^2$

Simplify: $2a^2 = 36 \rightarrow a^2 = 18 \rightarrow a = \sqrt{18}$

$a = \sqrt{18} \Rightarrow$ area of the triangle is $= \frac{1}{2}\left(\sqrt{18} \times \sqrt{18}\right) = \frac{1}{2} \times 18 = 9\ cm^2$

17) Choice B is correct

The area of the non-shaded region is equal to the area of the bigger rectangle subtracted by the area of smaller rectangle. Area of the bigger rectangle $= 12 \times 16 = 192$

Area of the smaller rectangle $= 10 \times 4 = 40$, Area of the non-shaded region $= 192 - 40 = 152$

18) Choice B is correct

$79.22 \div 0.05 = 1,584.4$

19) Choice B is correct

$3\frac{1}{3} - 2\frac{5}{6} = 3\frac{2}{6} - 2\frac{5}{6} = \frac{20}{6} - \frac{17}{6} = \frac{3}{6} = \frac{1}{2}$

20) Choice C is correct

Let's review the choices provided. Put the values of x and y in the equation.

A. $(1, 2)$ $\Rightarrow x = 1 \Rightarrow y = 2$ This is true!

B. $(-2, -13)$ $\Rightarrow x = -2 \Rightarrow y = -13$ This is true!

C. $(3, 18)$ $\Rightarrow x = 3 \Rightarrow y = 12$ This is not true!

D. $(2, 7)$ $\Rightarrow x = 2 \Rightarrow y = 7$ This is true!

21) Choice C is correct

To find total number of miles driven by Ed that week, you only need to subtract $40,907$ from $41,053$. $41,053 - 40,907 = 146\ miles$

22) Choice D is correct

To find the maximum value of y, the expression $(x - 2)^2$ must be equal to 0. Because it has a negative sign. Since $x - 2$ is to the power of 2, it cannot be negative. To get 0 for the expression $(x - 2)^2$, x must be 2. Plug in 2 for x in the equation: $y = -(x - 2)^2 + 6 \rightarrow y = -(2 - 2)^2 + 6 = 6$. The maximum value of y is 6.

23) Choice B is correct

$\begin{cases} -2x - y = -9 \\ 5x - 2y = 18 \end{cases} \Rightarrow$ Multiplication (-2) in first equation $\Rightarrow \begin{cases} 4x + 2y = 18 \\ 5x - 2y = 18 \end{cases}$

Add two equations together $\Rightarrow 9x = 36 \Rightarrow x = 4$ then: $y = 1$

24) Choice A is correct

First draw an isosceles triangle. Remember that two sides of the triangle are equal.

Let put a for the legs. Then:

$a = 6 \Rightarrow$ area of the triangle is $= \frac{1}{2}(6 \times 6) = \frac{36}{2} = 18 \; cm^2$

Isosceles right triangle

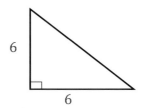

6

6

25) Choice A is correct

Factor each trinomial $x^2 - 2x - 8$ and $x^2 - 6x + 8$

$x^2 - 2x - 8 \Rightarrow (x - 4)(x + 2)$, $x^2 - 6x + 8 \Rightarrow (x - 2)(x - 4)$

The common factor of both expressions is $(x - 4)$.

26) Choice B is correct

$\frac{13}{25} = 0.52$

27) Choice C is correct

$x + y = 12$, Then: $8x + 8y = 8(x + y) = 8 \times 12 = 96$

28) Choice B is correct

$$\begin{array}{r} 37 \text{ hr. } 25 \text{ min.} \\ - 24 \text{ hr. } 38 \text{ min.} \\ \hline 12 \text{ hr. } 47 \text{ min} \end{array}$$

29) Choice C is correct

$\frac{450}{15} = 30 \; miles \; per \; gallon$

30) Choice C is correct

First, convert all measurement to foot. One foot is 12 inches. Then: 8 inches = $\frac{8}{12} = \frac{2}{3}$ feet

The volume flower box is: $length \times width \times height = 2 \times \frac{2}{3} \times 2 = \frac{8}{3}$ cubic feet.

31) Choice D is correct

$\frac{x^3}{16} \Rightarrow$ reciprocal is : $\frac{16}{x^3}$

32) Choice C is correct

Use interest rate formula: $Interest = principal \times rate \times time = 1,200 \times 0.05 \times 1 = \$60$

33) Choice D is correct

Ellis travels $\frac{3}{5}$ of 80 hours. $\frac{3}{5} \times 80 = 48$, Ellis will be on the road for 48 hours.

34) Choice A is correct

Plug in the values of x and y in the expression:

$2x^2(y + 4) = 2(0.6)^2(6 + 4) = 2(0.36)(10) = 7.2$

35) Choice B is correct

Let's write equations based on the information provided:

$Michelle = Karen - 9$

$Michelle = David - 4$

$Karen + Michelle + David = 82$

$Karen - 9 = Michelle \Rightarrow Karen = Michelle + 9$

$Karen + Michelle + David = 82$

Now, replace the ages of Karen and David by Michelle. Then:

$Michelle + 9 + Michelle + Michelle + 4 = 82$

$3Michelle + 13 = 82 \Rightarrow 3Michelle = 82 - 13$

$3Michelle = 69$

$Michelle = 23$

36) Choice C is correct

$A = bh, A = 2 \times 2.4 = 4.8 \; square \; feet$

37) Choice D is correct

To find the discount, multiply the number by $(100\% - rate\ of\ discount)$.

Therefore, for the first discount we get: $(200)(100\% - 25\%) = (200)(0.75)$

For the next 15% discount: $(200)(0.75)(0.85)$

38) Choice D is correct

The ratio of boys to girls is $3:7$. Therefore, there are 3 boys out of 10 students. To find the answer, first divide the number of boys by 3, then multiply the result by 10.

$180 \div 3 = 60 \Rightarrow 60 \times 10 = 600$

39) Choice A is correct

Write a proportion and solve for the missing number. $\frac{32}{12} = \frac{6}{x} \rightarrow 32x = 6 \times 12 = 72$

$32x = 72 \rightarrow x = \dfrac{72}{32} = 2.25\ ft$

40) Choice B is correct.

To find the area of the shaded region subtract smaller circle from bigger circle.

$S_{bigger} - S_{smaller} = \pi\left(r_{bigger}\right)^2 - \pi\left(r_{smaller}\right)^2 \Rightarrow S_{bigger} - S_{smaller} = \pi(6)^2 - \pi(4)^2 \Rightarrow 36\pi - 16\pi = 20\pi\ inch^2$

41) Choice C is correct.

To add two matrices, first we need to find corresponding members from each matrix.

$\begin{vmatrix} 3 & 6 \\ -1 & -3 \\ -5 & -1 \end{vmatrix} + \begin{vmatrix} 0 & -1 \\ 6 & 0 \\ 2 & 3 \end{vmatrix} = \begin{vmatrix} 3 & 5 \\ 5 & -3 \\ -3 & 2 \end{vmatrix}$

42) Choice C is correct

The area of a $18\ feet\ x\ 18\ feet$ room is 324 square feet. $18 \times 18 = 324$

43) Choice C is correct

Use FOIL (First, Out, In, Last). $(3x + 3)(x + 5) = 3x^2 + 15x + 3x + 15 = 3x^2 + 18x + 15$

44) Choice B is correct

Plug in the values of x and y in the equation: $5\blacksquare 11 = \sqrt{5^2 + 11} = \sqrt{25 + 11} = \sqrt{36} = 6$

45) Choice A is correct

Let x be the capacity of one tank. Then, $\frac{2}{5}x = 200 \to x = \frac{200 \times 5}{2} = 500$ Liters

The amount of water in three tanks is equal to: $3 \times 500 = 1,500$ Liters

46) Choice B is correct

$Average = \frac{sum\ of\ terms}{number\ of\ terms}$, The sum of the weight of all girls is: $18 \times 60 = 1,080\ kg$, The sum of the weight of all boys is: $32 \times 62 = 1,984\ kg$. The sum of the weight of all students is: $1,080 + 1,984 = 3,064\ kg$, $Average = \frac{3064}{50} = 61.28\ kg$

47) Choice B is correct

$\frac{45}{100} \times 820 = x$, $x = 369$, $x = 369$.

ISEE Upper Level Math Practice Test 2
Quantitative Reasoning

1) Choice D is correct

$2y + 6 < 30 \rightarrow 2y < 30 - 6 \rightarrow 2y < 24 \rightarrow y < 12$, Only choice D (8) is less than 12.

2) Choice C is correct

A factor must divide evenly into its multiple. 16 cannot be a factor of 90 because 90 divided by 16 = 5.625

3) Choice B is correct

The diagonal of the square is 6 meters. Let x be the side.

Use Pythagorean Theorem: $a^2 + b^2 = c^2$

$x^2 + x^2 = 6^2 \Rightarrow 2x^2 = 6^2 \Rightarrow 2x^2 = 36 \Rightarrow x^2 = 18 \Rightarrow x = \sqrt{18}$

The area of the square is: $\sqrt{18} \times \sqrt{18} = 18\ m^2$

4) Choice B is correct

To find what percent A is of B, divide A by B, then multiply that number by 100%:

$13.26 \div 58.56 = 0.2264 \times 100\% = 22.64\%$, This is approximately 22%.

5) Choice C is correct

$Probability = \dfrac{number\ of\ desired\ outcomes}{number\ of\ total\ outcomes}$

In this case, a desired outcome is selecting either a red or a yellow marble. Combine the number of red and yellow marbles: $9 + 6 = 15$, and divide this by the total number of marbles:

$7 + 9 + 6 = 22$. The probability is $\dfrac{15}{22}$.

6) Choice B is correct

Begin by calculating James's total earnings after 20 hours: $20\ hours \times \$8.500\ per\ hour = \$170$,Next, divide this total by Jacob's hourly rate to find the number of hours Jacob would need to work: $\$170 \div \$10.00\ per\ hour = 17\ hours$

7) Choice C is correct

The total cost of the phone call can be represented by the equation: $TC = \$5.00 + \$0.5x$, where x is the duration of the call after the first five minutes. In this case, $x = 30$. Substitute the known values into the equation and solve: $TC = \$5.00 + \$0.5 \times 30$

$TC = \$5.00 + \$15.00$, $TC = \$20.00$

8) Choice B is correct

Let b be the amount of time Alec can do the job, then,

$$\frac{1}{a} + \frac{1}{b} = \frac{1}{50} \rightarrow \frac{1}{150} + \frac{1}{b} = \frac{1}{50} \rightarrow \frac{1}{b} = \frac{1}{50} - \frac{1}{150} = \frac{2}{150} = \frac{1}{75}$$

Then: $b = 75$ minutes

9) Choice A is correct

First, find the number. Let x be the number. Write the equation and solve for x. 150% of a number is 75, then: $1.5 \times x = 75 \rightarrow x = 75 \div 1.5 = 50$, 90% of 50 is: $0.9 \times 50 = 45$

10) Choice B is correct

The length of MN is equal to: $4x + 6x = 10x$, Then: $10x = 50 \rightarrow x = \frac{50}{10} = 5$

The length of ON is equal to: $6x = 6 \times 5 = 30\ cm$

11) Choice A is correct

The distance on the map is proportional to the actual distance between the two cities. Use the information to set up a proportion and then solve for the unknown number of actual miles: $\frac{14\,miles}{\frac{1}{2}\,inches} = \frac{x\,miles}{18\,inches}$, Cross multiply and simplify to solve for the x:

$$\frac{14 \times 18}{\frac{1}{2}} = x\ miles \rightarrow \frac{252}{\frac{1}{2}} = 252 \times 2 = 504\ miles$$

12) Choice C is correct

Number of Mathematics books: $0.35 \times 700 = 245$

Number of English books: $0.13 \times 700 = 91$

Product of number of Mathematics and number of English books:

$$245 \times 91 = 22,295$$

13) Choice D is correct

If each book weighs $\frac{1}{6}$ pound, then $1\ pound = 6\ books$. To find the number of books in 60 pounds, simply multiply this 6 by 60: $60 \times 6 = 360$

14) Choice B is correct

Write equations based on the information provided in the question:

$Emily = Daniel, Emily = 6\ Claire, Daniel = 15 +\ Claire$

$Emily = Daniel\ \rightarrow Emily = 15 + Claire$

$Emily = 6\ Claire\ \rightarrow 6\ Claire = 15 + Claire \rightarrow 6\ Claire - Claire = 15$

$5\ Claire = 15, Claire = 3$

15) Choice A is correct

Begin by examining the sequence to find the pattern. The difference between 3 and 6 is 3; moving from 6 to 11 requires 5 to be added; moving from 11 to 18 requires 7 to be added. The pattern emerges here — adding by consecutive odd integers. The 5th term is equal to $18 + 9 = 27$, and the 6th term is equal to $27 + 11 = 38$.

16) Choice A is correct

The general slope-intercept form of the equation of a line is $y = mx + b$, where m is the slope and b is the y-intercept. By substitution of the given point and given slope: $-3 = (3)(2) + b$, So, $b = -3 - 6 = -9$, and the required equation is $y = 3x - 9$.

17) Choice D is correct

Multiplying each side of $-4x - y = 8$ by 2 gives $-8x - 2y = 16$. Adding each side of $-8x - 2y = 16$ to the corresponding side of $8x + 6y = 20$ gives $4y = 36$ or $y = 9$. Finally, substituting 9 for y in $8x + 6y = 20$ gives $8x + 6(9) = 20$ or $x = -\frac{17}{4}$.

18) Choice B is correct

The question is this: 530.20 is what percent of 631? Use percent formula:

$Part = \frac{percent}{100} \times whole,$

$530.20 = \frac{percent}{100} \times 631 \rightarrow 530.20 = \frac{percent \times 631}{100} \rightarrow 53020 = percent \times 631$

Then, $Percent = \frac{53020}{631} = 84.02$

530.20 is 84% of 631. Therefore, the discount is: $100\% - 84\% = 16\%$

19) Choice A is correct

Let x be the number. Write the equation and solve for x. $\frac{3}{2} \times 20 = \frac{5}{2}x \rightarrow \frac{3 \times 20}{2} = \frac{5x}{2}$, use cross multiplication to solve for x. $2 \times 60 = 5x \times 2 \Rightarrow 120 = 10x \Rightarrow x = 12$

20) Choice A is correct

Let's choose $100 for the sales of the supermarket. If the sales increases by 11 percent in April, the final amount of sales at the end of April will be $100 + (11\%) \times (\$100) = \$111$.

If sales then decreased by 11 percent in May, the final amount of sales at the end of August will be $\$111 - (\$111) \times (11\%) = \$98.79$

The final sales of $98 is 98% of the original price of $100. Therefore, the sales decreased by 2% overall.

21) Choice B is correct

The time it takes to drive from city A to city B is: $\frac{2700}{74} = 36.48$

22) Choice D is correct

First find the value of x in the equation: $x^2 = 8 \rightarrow x = \sqrt{8}$, or $x = -\sqrt{8}$. Since $\sqrt{8}$ is bigger than 2 and $-\sqrt{8}$ is smaller than 2. Then: the relationship cannot be determined from the information given.

23) Choice C is correct

Find the value of the functions in each column.

Column A: $4 \diamond 5 = 4^2 - 2(4)(5) + 5^2 = 16 - 40 + 25 = 1$,

Column B: $5 \diamond 4 = 5^2 - 2(5)(4) + 4^2 = 25 - 40 + 16 = 1$

The two quantities are equal

24) Choice B is correct

Column A: $\frac{16+22+24+36+40}{5} = \frac{138}{5} = 27.6$, Column B: $\frac{28+33+38+42}{4} = \frac{141}{4} = 35.25$

25) Choice D is correct

Let's plug in a value for x and compare the values in both columns.

$x = -1$

Column A: $\frac{1}{x+1} = \frac{1}{-1+1} = \frac{1}{0}$, this is undefined.

Column B: $\frac{2}{x+2} = \frac{2}{-1+2} = \frac{2}{1} = 2$

The relationship cannot be determined from the information given

26) Choice D is correct

First, solve the expression for x. $\frac{x}{3} = y^2 \rightarrow x = 3y^2$

Plug in different values for y and find the values of x.

Let's choose $y = 0 \rightarrow x = 3y^2 \rightarrow x = 3(0)^2 = 0$

The values in Column A and B are equal.

Now, let's choose $y = 1 \rightarrow x = 3y^2 \rightarrow x = 3(1)^2 = 3$

Column A is greater. So, the relationship cannot be determined from the information given.

27) Choice B is correct

Column A: $2x^3 - 3x - 2 = 2(1)^3 - 3(1) - 2 = 2 - 3 - 2 = -3$

Column B: $3x^2 - 2x - 3 = 3(1)^2 - 2(1) - 3 = 3 - 2 - 3 = -2$

28) Choice A is correct

Column A: $8 + 14(7 - 3) = 64$, Column B: $14 + 8(7 - 3) = 46$

29) Choice A is correct

First find the value of x. $\frac{x}{36} = \frac{3}{4} \rightarrow 4x = 3 \times 36 = 108 \rightarrow x = \frac{108}{4} = 27$

Column A: $\frac{9}{x} = \frac{9}{27} = \frac{1}{3}$

30) Choice C is correct

First convert hours to minutes. 3 hours 10 minutes $= 3 \times 60 + 10 = 190$ minutes.

Machine D makes b rolls of steel in 38 minutes. So, it makes 5 sets of b in 190 minutes.

$190 \div 38 = 5$ sets of b.

Machine E operates for 5 hours, making b rolls per hour. So, it makes a total of $5b$ rolls.

The two quantities are equal

31) Choice D is correct

$-1 < y < 4,$ Let's choose some values for y. $y = 1$

Column A: $\frac{y}{2} = \frac{1}{2}$, Column B: $\frac{2}{y} = \frac{2}{1} = 2$, In this case, column B is bigger.

$y = 3$, Column A: $\frac{y}{2} = \frac{3}{2}$, Column B: $\frac{2}{y} = \frac{2}{3}$

In this case, Column A is bigger. So, the relationship cannot be determined from the information given.

32) Choice D is correct

$\frac{a}{b} = \frac{c}{d}$, here there are two equal fractions. Let's choose some values for these variables. $\frac{1}{2} = \frac{2}{4}$

In this case, Column A is 3 $(1 + 2)$ and Column B is 6 $(2 + 4)$. Since, we can change the positions of these variables (for example put 2 for a and 4 for b), the relationship cannot be determined from the information given.

33) Choice A is correct

The ratio of boys to girls in a class is 5 to 7. Therefore, ratio of boys to the entire class is 5 out of 12. $\frac{5}{12} > \frac{1}{3}$

34) Choice B is correct

There are 9 marbles in the jar. Let's calculate each probability individually:

The probability that the first marble is blue $= \frac{4}{9}$

The probability that the second marble is blue $= \frac{3}{8}$

Column A: The probability that both marbles are blue $= \frac{4}{9} \times \frac{3}{8} = \frac{12}{72} = \frac{1}{6}$

The probability that the first marble is green $= \frac{5}{9}$

The probability that the second marble is blue $= \frac{4}{8} = \frac{1}{2}$

Column B: The probability that the first marbles is green, but the second is blue $= \frac{5}{9} \times \frac{1}{2} = \frac{5}{18}$

Column B is greater. $\frac{5}{18} > \frac{1}{6}$.

35) Choice A is correct

First, let's find the number of digits when the printer prints 100 pages.

If there are 2 digits in each page and the printer prints 100 pages, then, there will be 200 digits. $100 \times 2 = 200$

However, we know that pages $1 - 9$ have only one digit each, so we must subtract 9 from this total: $200 - 9 = 191$. We also know that the number 100th has three digits not two. So, we must add 1 digit to this total: $191 + 1 = 192$.

It is given that 195 digits were printed, and we know that 100 pages results in 192 digits total, so there must be 101 total pages in the magazine. Column A is greater.

36) Choice B is correct

Column A: The largest number that can be written by rearranging the digits in $381 = 831$

Column B: The largest number that can be written by rearranging the digits in $279 = 972$

37) Choice A is correct

The computer priced $147 includes 5% profit. Let x be the original cost of the computer.   Then: $x + 5\% \ of \ x = 147 \rightarrow x + 0.05x = 147 \rightarrow 1.05x = 147 \rightarrow x = \frac{147}{1.05} = \$140$

Column A is bigger.

ISEE Upper Level Math Practice Test 2
Mathematics Achievement

1) Choice A is correct.

$0.00003379 = \dfrac{3.379}{100,000} \Rightarrow 3.379 \times 10^{-5}$

2) Choice A is correct

$|10 - (12 \div |1 - 5|)| = |10 - (12 \div |-4|)| = |10 - (12 \div 4)| = |10 - 3| = |7| = 7$

3) Choice A is correct

Use FOIL (First, Out, In, Last) method.

$(x + 4)(x + 5) = x^2 + 5x + 4x + 20 = x^2 + 9x + 20$

4) Choice B is correct

Use quadratic formula: $ax^2 + bx + c = 0$

$x_{1,2} = \dfrac{-b \pm \sqrt{b^2 - 4ac}}{2a}$

$6x^2 + 16x + 8 \quad \Rightarrow \qquad$ then: $a = 6, b = 16$ and $c = 8$

$x = \dfrac{-16 + \sqrt{16^2 - 4 \times 6 \times 8}}{2 \times 6} = -\dfrac{2}{3}$

$x = \dfrac{-16 - \sqrt{16^2 - 4 \times 6 \times 8}}{2 \times 6} = -2$

5) Choice D is correct

Solve for x. $-2 \le 2x - 4 < 8 \Rightarrow$ (add 4 all sides) $-2 + 4 \le 2x - 4 + 4 < 8 + 4 \Rightarrow 2 \le 2x < 12 \Rightarrow$ (divide all sides by 2) $1 \le x < 6$. x is between 1 and 6. Choice D represent this inequality.

6) Choice C is correct

Simplify: $1 - 9 \div (4^2 \div 2) = -\dfrac{1}{8}$

7) Choice D is correct.

Write the proportion and solve for missing side.

$\dfrac{\text{Smaller triangle height}}{\text{Smaller triangle base}} = \dfrac{\text{Bigger triangle height}}{\text{Bigger triangle base}} \quad \Rightarrow \quad \dfrac{80cm}{200cm} = \dfrac{80 + 460cm}{x} \Rightarrow x = 1,350\ cm$

8) Choice D is correct.

First, notice that the line $-6y = 16x - 12$ has a negative slope. (graph the line and see that the line has a negative slope) Then, Choices B and C that show the line with positive slope are incorrect.

Now, choose the testing point $(0,0)$ and plug in the values of x and y in the inequality.

$$(0,0) \rightarrow -6y \leq 16x - 12 \rightarrow -6(0) \leq 16(0) - 12 \rightarrow 0 \leq -12$$

Number 0 is not less than -12. Then, the testing point $(0,0)$ is not in the solution section.

Therefore, choices A and B are incorrect. (notice that both graphs of A and B show the

testing point $(0,0)$ in the solution section.)

Only choice D represents the inequality $-6y \leq 16x - 12$

9) Choice B is correct

The ratio of boy to girls is $3:5$. Therefore, there are 3 boys out of 8 students. To find the answer, first divide the total number of students by 8, then multiply the result by 3.

$600 \div 8 = 75 \Rightarrow 75 \times 3 = 225$

10) Choice D is correct

$90 \div \dfrac{1}{9} = 90 \times 9 = 810$

11) Choice B is correct.

Translated 5 units down and 4 units to the left means: $(x.y) \Rightarrow (x - 4, y - 5)$

12) Choice A is correct

Area of a rectangle $= width \times height,\ Area\ = 148 \times 90 = 1,3320\ sq.ft$

13) Choice C is correct.

$\dfrac{4}{23} = 0.173$ and $25\% = 0.25$ therefore x should be between 0.173 and 0.25. Only

choice B ($\sqrt{0.044}$)$= 0.20$ is between 0.173 and 0.25.

14) Choice D is correct

Some of prime numbers are: $2, 3, 5, 7, 11, 13$. Find the product of two consecutive prime numbers: $2 \times 3 = 6$ (not in the options), $3 \times 5 = 15$ (bingo!), $5 \times 7 = 35$ (not in the options)

15) Choice B is correct

The perimeter of the trapezoid is 38 cm. Therefore, the missing side is:

$38 - 13 - 9 - 4 = 12$. Area of a trapezoid: $A = \frac{1}{2}h(b_1 + b_2) = \frac{1}{2}(12)(4 + 9) = 78$

16) Choice A is correct

$\frac{1}{2}$ of the distance $4\frac{1}{5}$ miles is: $\frac{1}{2} \times 4\frac{1}{5} = \frac{1}{2} \times \frac{21}{5} = \frac{21}{10}$, Converting $\frac{21}{10}$ to a mixed number gives: $\frac{21}{10} = 2\frac{1}{10}$

17) Choice B is correct

$$average = \frac{sum}{total} = \frac{40 + 45 + 50}{3} = \frac{135}{3} = 45 \; miles$$

18) Choice B is correct

Use Pythagorean theorem: $a^2 + b^2 = c^2 \rightarrow s^2 + h^2 = (3s)^2 \rightarrow s^2 + h^2 = 9s^2$

Subtracting s^2 from both sides gives: $h^2 = 8s^2$

Square roots of both sides: $h = \sqrt{8s^2} = \sqrt{4 \times 2 \times s^2} = \sqrt{4} \times \sqrt{2} \times \sqrt{s^2} = 2 \times s \times \sqrt{2} = 2s\sqrt{2}$

19) Choice C is correct

Let x be the number of purple marbles. Let's review the choices provided:

A. $\frac{1}{11}$, if the probability of choosing a purple marble is one out of ten, then:

$$Probability = \frac{number \; of \; desired \; outcomes}{number \; of \; total \; outcomes} = \frac{x}{40+40+30+x} = \frac{1}{11}$$

Use cross multiplication and solve for x. $11x = 110 + x \rightarrow 10x = 110 \rightarrow x = 11$

Since, number of purple marbles can be 9, then, choice be the probability of randomly selecting a purple marble from the bag.

Use same method for other choices.

B. $\frac{1}{6}$

$$\frac{x}{40+40+30+x} = \frac{1}{6} \rightarrow 6x = 110 + x \rightarrow 5x = 110 \rightarrow x = 22$$

C. $\frac{2}{5}$

$$\frac{x}{40+40+30+x} = \frac{2}{5} \rightarrow 5x = 220 + 2x \rightarrow 3x = 220 \rightarrow x = 73.3$$

D. $\frac{1}{23}$

$$\frac{x}{40+40+30+x} = \frac{1}{23} \rightarrow 23x = 110 + x \rightarrow 22x = 110 \rightarrow x = 5$$

Number of purple marbles cannot be a decimal.

20) Choice C is correct

Let x be the original price of the dress. Then: 23% of $x = 21.87$

$$x = \frac{23}{100}x = 21.87 , x = \frac{100 \times 21.87}{23} \cong 95.09$$

21) Choice D is correct

$$\frac{8}{35} = 0.228$$

22) Choice B is correct

30% of A is 1,200 Then: $0.3A = 1,200 \rightarrow A = \frac{1,200}{0.3} = 4,000$

12% of 4,000 is: $0.12 \times 4,000 = 480$

23) Choice D is correct

Simplify:

$$\frac{\frac{1}{3}-\frac{x-4}{9}}{\frac{x^3}{3}-\frac{7}{3}}=\frac{\frac{1}{3}-\frac{x-4}{9}}{\frac{x^3-7}{3}}=\frac{3(\frac{1}{3}-\frac{x-4}{9})}{x^3-7}$$

$\Rightarrow$ Simplify: $\frac{1}{3}-\frac{x-4}{9}=\frac{7-x}{9}$

Then: $\frac{3(\frac{7-x}{9})}{x^3-7}=\frac{\frac{7-x}{3}}{x^3-7}=\frac{7-x}{3(x^3-7)}=\frac{7-x}{3x^3-21}$

24) Choice A is correct

$(6.2+8.3+2.4)\times x=x$, $16.9x=x$, Then: $x=0$

25) Choice B is correct

For sum of 5: $(1\ \&\ 4)$ *and* $(4\ \&\ 1),(2\ \&\ 3)$ and $(3\ \&\ 2)$, therefore we have 4 options.

For sum of 8: $(5\ \&\ 3)$ *and* $(3\ \&\ 5),(4\ \&\ 4)$ and $(2\ \&\ 6),(6\ \&\ 2)$, we have 5 options. To get a sum of 5 or 8 for two dice: $4+5=9$

Since, we have $6\times6=36$ total number of options, the probability of getting a sum of 5 and 8 is 9 out of 36 or $\frac{9}{36}=\frac{1}{4}$

26) Choice C is correct

Write a proportion and solve. $\frac{7}{38}=\frac{x}{190}\rightarrow x=\frac{7\times190}{38}=35$

27) Choice B is correct

$78.56\div0.05=1,571.2$

28) Choice D is correct

The distance of A to B on the coordinate plane is: $\sqrt{(x_1-x_2)^2+(y_1-y_2)^2}=\sqrt{(2-10)^2+(6-12)^2}=\sqrt{8^2+6^2},=\sqrt{64+36}=\sqrt{100}=10$

The diameter of the circle is 10 and the radius of the circle is 5. Then: the circumference of the circle is: $2\pi r=2\pi(5)=10\pi$

29) Choice C is correct

$2x^2+6=26\rightarrow2x^2=20\rightarrow x^2=10\rightarrow x=\pm\sqrt{10}$

30) Choice A is correct

Diameter $=20$, then: Radius $=10$, Area of a circle $=\pi r^2\Rightarrow A=3.14(10)^2=314$

31)Choice A is correct

$6\ days\ 20\ hours\ 36\ minutes\ -\ 4\ days\ 12\ hours\ 24\ minutes\ =$
$2\ days\ 8\ hours\ 12minutes$

32)Choice C is correct

Formula of triangle area $= \frac{1}{2}(base \times height)$. Since the angles are $45-45-90$, then this is an isosceles triangle, meaning that the base and height of the triangle are equal.

$Triangle\ area\ =\ \frac{1}{2}\ (base \times height) = \frac{1}{2}(4 \times 4) = 8\ square\ feet$

33)Choice B is correct

The mean of the data is 11. Then: $\frac{x+10+15+13+6}{5} = 11 \rightarrow x\ +\ 44\ =\ 55 \rightarrow x\ = 55 - 44 = 11$

34)Choice C is correct

The difference of the file added, and the file deleted is:

$542,159 - 499,986\ =\ 42,173$ bytes

$837,036 + 42,173\ =\ 879,209$ bytes

35)Choice B is correct

$40\%\ of\ 70\ = 28 \rightarrow 70 + 28 = 98$

36)Choice D is correct

$x^{\frac{1}{2}}$equals to the root of x. Then: $12 + x^{\frac{1}{2}} = 24 \rightarrow 12 + \sqrt{x} = 24 \rightarrow \sqrt{x} = 12 \rightarrow x = 144$

$x\ = 144$ and $5 \times x$ equals: $5 \times 144 = 720$

37)Choice C is correct

Only choice C represents the statement "twice the difference between 5 times H and 2 gives 35". $2(5H - 2)\ =\ 35$

38)Choice D is correct

The area of the circle is $25\pi\ cm^2$, then, its diameter is $10cm$. $area\ of\ a\ circle = \pi r^2 = 25\pi \rightarrow r^2 = 25 \rightarrow r = 5\ cm$ .Radius of the circle is 5 and diameter is twice of it, 10.One side of the square equals to the diameter of the circle. Then:$Area\ of\ square = side \times side = 10 \times 10 = 100\ cm^2$

39) Choice C is correct.

When a point is reflected over x axes, the (y) coordinate of that point changes to $(-y)$ while its x coordinate remains the same. C $(9, 7) \rightarrow$ C' $(9, -7)$

40) Choice D is correct.

A set of ordered pairs represents y as a function of x if: $x_1 = x_2 \rightarrow y_1 = y_2$

In choice A: $(5, -2)$ and $(5, 7)$ are ordered pairs with same x and different y, therefore y isn't a function of x.

In choice B: $(2, 2)$ and $(2, 7)$ are ordered pairs with same x and different y, therefore y isn't a function of x.

In choice C: $(8, 7)$ and $(8, 18)$ are ordered pairs with same x and different y, therefore y isn't a function of x.

41) Choice D is correct

If the length of the box is $24\ cm$, then the width of the box is one third of it, $8\ cm$, and the height of the box is $4\ cm$ (half of the width). The volume of the box is:

$V = length \times width \times height = (24)(8)(4) = 768\ cm^3$

42) Choice D is correct

Number of squares equal to: $\frac{40 \times 12}{4 \times 4} = 10 \times 3 = 30$

43) Choice A is correct

David's weekly salary is $230 plus 9% of $1,200. Then: $9\%\ of\ 1,200 = 0.09 \times 1,200 = 108$

$230 + 108 = 338$

44) Choice B is correct

$5x^3 y^{\,2} + 4x^5 y^{\,3} - (6x^3 y^2 - 4xy^5) = 5x^3 y^{\,2} + 4x^5 y^{\,3} - 6x^3 y^2 + 4xy^5) = 4x^5 y^3 - x^3 y^2 + 4xy^5$

45) Choice B is correct

Let P be circumference of circle A, then; $2\pi r_A = 20\pi \rightarrow r_A = 10$

$r_A = 5r_B \rightarrow r_B = \frac{10}{5} = 2 \rightarrow$ Area of circle B is; $\pi r_B^2 = 4\pi$

46) Choice D is correct

The area of the square is 64 square inches. *Area of square = side × side =* $8 \times 8 = 64 \ inch^2$

The length of the square is increased by 5 inches and its width decreased by 4 inches. Then, its area equals: *Area of rectangle = width × length =* $13 \times 4 = 52$

The area of the square will be decreased by 12 square inches. $64 - 52 = 12$

47) Choice D is correct

Write a proportion and solve. $\frac{3}{2} = \frac{x}{80}$, Use cross multiplication: $2x = 240 \rightarrow x = 120$

Effortless Math's ISEE Upper Level Online Center

... So Much More Online!

Effortless Math Online ISEE Upper Level Math Center offers a complete study program, including the following:

✓ Step-by-step instructions on how to prepare for the ISEE Upper Level Math test

✓ Numerous ISEE Upper Level Math worksheets to help you measure your math skills

✓ Complete list of ISEE Upper Level Math formulas

✓ Video lessons for ISEE Upper Level Math topics

✓ Full-length ISEE Upper Level Math practice tests

✓ And much more...

No Registration Required.

Visit **EffortlessMath.com/ISEE** to find your online ISEE Upper Level Math resources.

Receive the PDF version of this book or get another FREE book!

Thank you for using our Book!

Do you LOVE this book?

Then, you can get the PDF version of this book or another book absolutely FREE!

Please email us at:

info@EffortlessMath.com

for details.

Author's Final Note

I hope you enjoyed reading this book. You've made it through the book! Great job!

First of all, thank you for purchasing this study guide. I know you could have picked any number of books to help you prepare for your ISEE Upper Level Math test, but you picked this book and for that I am extremely grateful.

It took me years to write this study guide for the ISEE Upper Level Math because I wanted to prepare a comprehensive ISEE Upper Level Math study guide to help test takers make the most effective use of their valuable time while preparing for the test.

After teaching and tutoring math courses for over a decade, I've gathered my personal notes and lessons to develop this study guide. It is my greatest hope that the lessons in this book could help you prepare for your test successfully.

If you have any questions, please contact me at reza@effortlessmath.com and I will be glad to assist. Your feedback will help me to greatly improve the quality of my books in the future and make this book even better. Furthermore, I expect that I have made a few minor errors somewhere in this study guide. If you think this to be the case, please let me know so I can fix the issue as soon as possible.

If you enjoyed this book and found some benefit in reading this, I'd like to hear from you and hope that you could take a quick minute to post a review on the book's Amazon page. To leave your valuable feedback, please visit: amzn.to/3fPW03O

Or scan this QR code.

I personally go over every single review, to make sure my books really are reaching out and helping students and test takers. Please help me help ISEE Upper Level Math test takers, by leaving a review!

I wish you all the best in your future success!

Reza Nazari

Math teacher and author

Made in the USA
Middletown, DE
11 March 2024